MR. & MRS.
JOHN CHRISTIAN WILSON

5/1/72

Peter's Pentecost Discourse

Peter's Pentecost Discourse

Tradition and Lukan Reinterpretation
in Peter's Speeches of Acts 2 and 3

Richard F. Zehnle

Society of Biblical Literature
Monograph Series
15
Robert A. Kraft, Editor

Published for the
Society of Biblical Literature

by

Abingdon Press

Nashville ♪ New York

PETER'S PENTECOST DISCOURSE

ISBN 0-687-20629-4

Library of Congress Catalog Card Number: 72-148063

SET UP, PRINTED, AND BOUND BY THE
PARTHENON PRESS, AT NASHVILLE,
TENNESSEE, UNITED STATES OF AMERICA

I should like to extend a special word of thanks to Père M. E. Boismard, who provided inspiration and direction in the early stages of this work; to Robert A. Kraft, editor of the monograph series, for his competent and helpful criticism in the later stages; to Mrs. Susan Philipps, who typed the successive drafts; and to my wife, whose patience and encouragement saw a long (and sometimes tedious) labor to its conclusion.

This work is dedicated

TO

MY PARENTS

IN LOVE AND GRATITUDE

Contents

Special Terminology

In this study, the phrase "early Christian literature" is used in two ways: (1) for questions concerning the style and vocabulary of Luke-Acts, it refers to the works encompassed by the Bauer-Arndt-Gingrich *Lexicon* (see p. 57 n. 115), and to the evidence cited therein; (2) for the study of the use of titles, exegetical traditions, and concepts, however, later literature such as the works of Justin and the pseudo-Clementine material has been consulted for whatever light it may throw on earlier developments.

Contemporary research on Jewish scriptural materials available in Greek in the ancient world indicates that a variety of translation techniques made their influence felt in the early centuries of the common era, both in Jewish and in Christian circles. The collection of Greek scriptures that has come to be known as "the Septuagint" is by no means a homogeneous translation, but includes materials produced over a relatively long period of time, and perhaps also in different locations, by a variety of persons or groups who had varying approaches to their task.[1] Furthermore, prior to the development of the large-scale codex in the late third and early fourth century of the common era, writings circulated mostly in the form of rolls or of small codices with rather limited content. This also makes it difficult to speak with any precision about a Greek "bible" in the later sense of a single volume in which a large corpus of "scriptural" (canonical) materials was collected and circulated. Although the term "Septuagint" can perhaps be applied to the old Greek form of the Pentateuch with some historical and philological justification, there would seem to be little value for the historian in using the same term simplistically also to cover the other writings that later came to be included in collections of Jewish Greek scriptures—as though the term referred to a single, concrete work of translation. Rather, for the following discussion, "Septuagint" (LXX) will be reserved for the earliest ascertainable Pentateuch text in Greek, while for other portions of "Greek Jewish scriptures," phrases like the "old Greek" version (e.g. of Joel, Psalms) will be used to refer to the earliest ascertainable Greek forms.

---

[1] For a recent discussion of many of these problems, see Sidney Jellicoe, *The Septuagint and Modern Study* (Oxford: Clarendon Press, 1968), especially 314*ff*.

Abbreviations

1. *Primary Sources:*
   The abbreviations used for Jewish and Christian canonical scriptures (including the apocrypha) are those found in *A Manual of Style*, 12th ed. rev. (Chicago: University of Chicago Press, 1969), 328-30. For standard editions of early Christian literature, see the lists in *A Patristic Greek Lexicon*, ed. G. W. H. Lampe (New York: Oxford University Press, 1969).

Barn	The Epistle of Barnabas
1-2 Clem	First and Second Clement
Did	Didache
Herm	The Shepherd of Hermas, for which both the new text divisions and the old (Mandates, Similitudes, Visions) are provided.
Hom	Pseudo-Clementine Homilies
Josephus, Antiq	The Antiquities of the Jews
_____, War	The Jewish War
4 Macc	The Fourth Book of the Maccabees
Mart Pol	The Martyrdom of Polycarp
Pol	The Epistle of Polycarp to the Philippians
Rec	Pseudo-Clementine Recognitions

2. *Periodicals, Series, and Reference Works:*

Beginnings	F. J. Foakes-Jackson and Kirsopp Lake, eds., The Beginnings of Christianity. Part I. The Acts of the Apostles, 5 vols. (London: Macmillan & Co., 1920-1935)
CBQ	Catholic Biblical Quarterly
ETL	Ephemerides Theologicae Lovanienses
EvT	Evangelische Theologie

ExpT	Expository Times
Hennecke- Schneemelcher	New Testament Apocrypha, ed. E. Hen- necke and W. Schneemelcher, trans. ed. R. McL. Wilson, 2 vols. (Philadel- phia: Westminster Press, 1963–65)
JBL	Journal of Biblical Literature
JTS	Journal of Theological Studies
NovT	Novum Testamentum
NTS	New Testament Studies
RB	Revue Biblique
Rech Bib	Recherches Bibliques
RHPhilRel	Revue d'Histoire et de Philosophie Re- ligieuses
S-B	H. Strack and P. Billerbeck, Kommentar zum Neuen Testament aus Talmud und Midrasch, 4 vols. (Munich: Beck, 1922-24)
SBT	Studies in Biblical Theology (London: SCM Press)
ST	Studia Theologica
Studies in Luke-Acts	Studies in Luke-Acts, eds. Leander E. Keck and J. Louis Martyn (Nashville: Abingdon Press, 1966)
TDNT	Theological Dictionary of the New Tes- tament, ed. Gerhard Kittel, trans. Geoffrey Bromiley, vols. 1–6 (Grand Rapids: Eerdmans, 1964–68)
TS	Theological Studies
TU	Texte und Untersuchungen zur Ge- schichte der altchristlichen Literatur (Berlin: Akademie Verlag)
WMANT	Wissenschaftliche Monographien zum Alten und Neuen Testament (Neu- kirchen-Vluyn: Neukirchener Verlag)
ZNW	Zeitschrift für die neutestamentliche Wissenschaft und die Kunde des alten Christentums
ZTK	Zeitschrift für Theologie und Kirche

Introduction

Only within the last fifty years has critical research into the Acts of the Apostles given special consideration to the study of the speeches of Acts themselves. Previous research, whether of the *Tendenzkritik* or *Quellenkritik* variety, tended to regard the speeches as simply one part of the whole among others.[1] Though principles for the future study of the discourses were perceived and elucidated, no works were specifically dedicated to the problem of these discourses in themselves.

The great pioneer of modern Acts criticism in Germany was Martin Dibelius. Although his definitive study of the speeches in Acts did not appear until 1949, the principles crystallized at that time were laid down in earlier works: *Die Formgeschichte des Evangeliums* (1919)[2] and "Stilkritisches zur Apostelgeschichte" (1923).[3] Dibelius claimed for the author of Acts (who shall be hereafter designated "Luke") a great liberty in the construction of the discourses, in the manner of the great Greek historians. But he realized that Luke as proclaimer

[1] An excellent history of Acts criticism can be found in Ernst Haenchen, *Die Apostelgeschichte*, 5th ed. rev., Kritisch-exegetischer Kommentar über das Neue Testament, 3 (Göttingen: Vandenhoeck and Ruprecht, 1965), 13-46. See also the studies by Jacques Dupont: *Les Problèmes du Livre des Actes d'après les travaux récents* (Louvain: Publications Universitaires, 1950), which may now be found in *Études sur les Actes des Apôtres*, Lectio Divina 45 (Paris: Cerf, 1967), 11-124; and *The Sources of Acts*, trans. Kathleen Pond (New York: Herder and Herder, 1964). For a discussion of the literature on the speeches themselves, see Ulrich Wilckens, *Die Missionsreden der Apostelgeschichte*, WMANT 5 (1963, 2nd ed.), 7-30.

[2] A second, revised edition of this book appeared in 1933 (Tübingen: Mohr), and served as the basis for the English translation by B. L. Woolf entitled *From Tradition to Gospel* (New York: Scribner's, 1935). In 1959, G. Bornkamm edited a reprint of the second German edition, with an appended note by G. Iber.

[3] Contained in Martin Dibelius, *Studies in the Acts of the Apostles*, trans. Mary Ling (New York: Scribner's, 1956), pp. 1-25. The 1949 essay, "The Speeches in Acts and Ancient Historiography," is on pp. 138-85. In *Gnomon* 25 (1953), 497-506, A. D. Nock, although holding against Dibelius that the author of Acts was an actual travel-companion of Paul, commends the studies highly, especially the analysis of the discourses: "If Dibelius is helpful and suggestive on other aspects of Acts, he is at his best on the speeches" (p. 503). C. K. Barrett, *Luke the Historian in Recent Study* (London: Epworth Press, 1961), reviews the work of Dibelius and five later exegetes, including two who were critical of Dibelius. Barrett basically accepts the judgment of Dibelius on the speeches (see especially pp. 68f.).

of the Christian message had placed himself within the framework of the evangelical tradition. By demonstrating the two forces at work in the discourses, Lukan composition and evangelical tradition, Dibelius contributed not so much a conclusion to research into the speeches as a beginning. Identifying what exactly in the speeches reflects the original composition and theological insights of Luke and what reflects traditions of the early community would be a task for those who would follow him in Acts research.

At the same time in America, another scholar was coming to similar conclusions. Henry J. Cadbury published an essay in 1922, "The Greek and Jewish Traditions of Writing History," [4] which found Luke (and Josephus) in the tradition not only of Greek historiographers, but also of Jewish historians such as the Chronicler, who did not scruple to add speeches where he felt them necessary. Cadbury developed and defended his thesis in *The Making of Luke-Acts* (1927) and "The Speeches in Acts" (1935). [5] The latter decisively refutes the assumption that the discourses were actually given by the speakers and on the occasions indicated by the Acts. But a later work, *The Book of Acts in History* (1955), detected in the speeches in Acts a considerable acquaintance with Jewish culture, especially with the rabbinic exegetical principle of seeing references to the messiah in scriptural passages which ostensibly refer to someone else. Such an acquaintance with the Jewish and Jewish Christian world certainly must be considered in deciding the question of sources and the composition of the speeches.

In 1936, C. H. Dodd attempted to isolate as a primitive element in the speeches of Acts a common schema, which was attributed to the early kerygma of the community. [6] After a hasty and somewhat superficial review of the New Testament evidence, he concluded: "A comparison, then, of the Pauline epistles with the speeches in Acts leads to a fairly clear and certain outline sketch of the preaching of the apostles" (31).

At first Dodd's hypothesis won the field. It was accepted by F. F. Bruce,[7] W. L. Knox,[8] J. Schmitt,[9] and E. Trocmé,[10] the last-mentioned

---

[4] *Beginnings* 2, 7-29.

[5] (New York: The Macmillan Co., 1927); *Beginnings* 5, 402-27.

[6] *The Apostolic Preaching and Its Developments* (New York: Harper, 1936).

[7] *The Speeches in Acts* (London: Tyndale Press, 1942), 27.

[8] *The Acts of the Apostles* (Cambridge: The University Press, 1948), 17.

[9] *Jésus Réssuscité dans la prédication apostolique* (Paris: Gabalda, 1949). No explicit reference is made to Dodd.

[10] *Le "Livre des Acts" et l'Histoire,* Études d'Histoire et de Philosophie Reli-

going so far as to criticize Cadbury for not having noted the schema. But in 1956 a thoroughgoing critique of Dodd's theses was provided by C. F. Evans,[11] in an article which reopened the question of the speeches and paved the way for the work of Wilckens and J. A. T. Robinson.

While Dodd was able to brand the kerygma of Acts as "pretheological" as late as 1952,[12] German scholars were establishing beyond doubt the originality and force of the proper theological conceptions of the author of Acts. P. Vielhauer raised the question of the possibility of a properly Lukan theology in his article, "Zum 'Paulinismus' der Apostelgeschichte." [13] H. Conzelmann's monumental *Die Mitte der Zeit* appeared in 1953 [14] and marked a "turning point" [15] in Acts study, along with the commentary of E. Haenchen, first published in 1956 (see n. 1). Henceforth, criticism of the speeches in Acts would have to reckon with the factor of the proper theological conceptions of Luke, conceptions which are more evident in Acts than in the third gospel because of the greater originality required in the plan.

The stage was set for a thoroughgoing literary analysis of the speeches in Acts with the question of Luke's proper theological position in view. The first response to this need was the *Habilitationsschrift* of U. Wilckens, *Die Missionsreden der Apostelgeschichte,* which first appeared in 1961 (see n. 1). After a detailed analysis of the "mission discourses" [16] in Acts, he concluded that they were summaries of Luke's own theological outlook. They are not to be understood as witnesses to an early or to the earliest primitive Christian theology, but as Lukan theology of the end of the first century. There are certainly good traditions behind the work of Luke, but he has created a unified theological picture out of the materials he received. Far from the

gieuses . . . de Strasbourg 45 (Paris: Presses Universitaires de France, 1957), 208.

[11] "The Kerygma," *JTS* 7 (1956), 25-41.

[12] *According to the Scriptures* (New York: Scribner's, 1952), 12.

[13] *EvT* 5 (1950/1951), 1ff. English translation: "On the 'Paulinism' of Acts," trans. Wm. C. Robinson, Jr. and Victor P. Furnish, *Studies in Luke-Acts,* 33-50.

[14] References are to the English translation: *The Theology of St. Luke,* trans. Geoffrey Buswell (New York: Harper, 1960).

[15] W. C. van Unnik, "Luke-Acts, a Storm Center in Contemporary Scholarship," *Studies in Luke-Acts,* 23.

[16] Under this rubric Wilckens designates the six addresses in the first part of Acts in which the chief apostles (Peter or Paul) proclaim the Christian message to their Jewish audience: Acts 2:14-39; 3:12-26; 4:9-12; 5:30-32; 10:34-43; 13:16-38. Other speeches (4:24-30; 14:15-17; 17:22-31) are taken into consideration, but Peter's first address to the disciples (1:15-26) and Stephen's speech (7:2-53) are omitted.

literary drudge he was suspected of being, Luke emerges as a creative theologian.[17]

A different line of investigation was taken by J. A. T. Robinson in his 1956 article, "The Most Primitive Christology of All?" [18] Robinson finds two incompatible christologies in the speeches of Acts 2 and 3, neither of which is the christology of Luke. The latter represents the earliest christology of all,[19] in which Jesus is still only the Christ-elect and the messianic age has still to be inaugurated.

J. C. O'Neill challenged Robinson's claim that the christology of the speech of Acts 2 is pre-Lukan,[20] but admitted that in the speech of Acts 3, "Luke may be passing on primitive material" (128). However, in his view the speech of Acts 3 is a Lukan composition as are all the speeches. If it has a different christological viewpoint it is because Luke "has designed the speech to fit perfectly into the developing pattern of Acts" (129).

The notion of Luke's awareness of development in the materials he used, and the search for his theology "primarily in the movement of his history" (71f.) is O'Neill's most significant contribution to the criticism of the speeches of Acts according to Conzelmann.[21] O'Neill, as Wilckens, arrives at the conclusion that what is advanced in the speeches is Luke's own theological viewpoint, though there are fairly certain indications that primitive materials have been used. Wilckens insists that Luke has created from disparate material a unified picture of the theology of the community from its earliest times to his own day. O'Neill adds the thesis that Luke has also created a series of glimpses as to how that theology developed.[22]

This brief résumé of recent critical inquiry into the speeches of Acts reveals widespread agreement on two points: First, there is a Lukan theology which orders and directs the author's two-volume work; second, Luke has used disparate materials in constructing his work. These are obviously not contradictory statements, but they

---

[17] *Missionsreden,* 189. J. Dupont's lengthy critique offers a valuable corrective: "Les Discours Missionnaires des Actes des Apôtres," *RB* 69 (1962), 37-60.

[18] *JTS* 7 (1956), 177-89.

[19] Defended in his book, *Jesus and His Coming* (London: SCM Press, 1957).

[20] J. C. O'Neill, *The Theology of Acts* (London: SPCK, 1961), 124-27.

[21] "Luke's Place in the Development of Early Christianity," *Studies in Luke-Acts,* 309.

[22] This suggestion was already advanced by Cadbury, *Making,* 325. Dodd, *Apostolic Preaching,* 19, summarily dismissed "deliberate archaism" as impossible for Luke, which is strange for one who claims that the same author has reproduced a primitive kerygma schema.

16

define the tension existing in Acts research today: Has Luke so re-worked his material that any detectable theological viewpoint in Acts must be said to be properly his? Or can elements of a primitive theology be found in the speeches of Acts, whether it be a kerygmatic schema (Dodd), or an embryonic christology (Robinson)? In short, does the book of Acts provide any identifiable material for the study of the development of the christology of the early community?

The present work concentrates on the first two "mission discourses" of Acts, namely the Petrine speeches of Acts 2 and 3. In successive chapters the speeches are studied in the light of (1) their literary composition, (2) their thought content, and (3) their role in the development of the book of Acts as a whole. It will be maintained that the speech of Acts 2 is the "keynote address" [23] of Acts, a summary statement of the theological viewpoint of the author from which the subsequent unfolding of the book is to be understood, but that the speech of Acts 3 reproduces primitive conceptions with a fidelity that affords an important glimpse of an early stage of the theological development of the community.

---

[23] Borrowing a phrase from Cadbury, *Making,* 188—which he used to describe the address in the synagogue of Nazareth (Luke 4:17-28).

1. Literary Composition of the Speeches

This chapter analyzes the discourses of chapters 2 and 3 according to the elements which make up the discourses, the literary structure into which these elements have been organized, and the vocabulary and style in which they are presented. The other discourses, especially the early mission discourses, will also be considered for the light they can throw on this analysis.

The Discourses of Chapters 2 and 3: Similarity

When the first two mission discourses of Peter in Acts are analyzed into their component elements, their resemblance is striking. The Greek texts of these speeches have been reproduced in the following pages.[1] Anticipating a later conclusion, the speech of Acts 3 is transcribed in the left-hand column—as the earlier composition. Corresponding elements from the speech of Acts 2 are given in the right hand column.[2] With one exception (#6), there is a corresponding element in the discourse of Acts 2 for every element from Acts 3.

1. The most common salutation in Acts, ἄνδρες, begins each discourse.

	2:14. ἄνδρες 'Ιουδαῖοι καὶ οἱ κατοι-κοῦντες 'Ιερουσαλὴμ πάντες
3:12b. ἄνδρες 'Ισραηλῖται	2:22. ἄνδρες 'Ισραηλῖται
	2:29. ἄνδρες ἀδελφοί

2. The speaker begins by correcting a false impression among his hearers, which also serves to connect the discourse to the preceding event.

---

[1] The text of Nestle's 25th edition is reproduced here. Important variant readings affecting passages essential to the development of the argument will be considered as the occasion arises.

[2] As will be seen, this comparison differs in many respects from that of Eduard Schweizer, "Zu den Reden der Apostelgeschichte," *Theologische Zeitschrift* 13 (1957), 1-11. (Eng.: "Concerning the Speeches in Acts," *Studies in Luke-Acts* pp. 186-93). The disagreement can be explained from a difference of method (Schweizer uses the speech of chapter 2 as a norm for the other speeches), and partly from a

3:12b. Τί θαυμάζετε ἐπὶ τούτῳ, ἢ ἡμῖν τί ἀτενίζετε ὡς ἰδίᾳ δυνάμει ἢ εὐσεβείᾳ πεποιηκόσιν τοῦ περιπατεῖν αὐτόν;

2:14-15. τοῦτο ὑμῖν γνωστὸν ἔστω, καὶ ἐνωτίσασθε τὰ ῥήματά μου. οὐ γὰρ ὡς ὑμεῖς ὑπολαμβάνετε οὗτοι μεθύουσιν, ἔστιν γὰρ ὥρα τρίτη τῆς ἡμέρας.

3. The speaker solemnly declares that God has glorified Jesus, whom the hearers had rejected.

2:36. ἀσφαλῶς οὖν γινωσκέτω πᾶς οἶκος Ἰσραὴλ

3:13-14. ὁ θεὸς Ἀβραὰμ καὶ Ἰσαὰκ καὶ Ἰακώβ, ὁ θεὸς τῶν πατέρων ἡμῶν, ἐδόξασεν τὸν παῖδα αὐτοῦ Ἰησοῦν, ὃν ὑμεῖς μὲν παρεδώκατε καὶ ἠρνήσασθε κατὰ πρόσωπον Πιλάτου, κρίναντος ἐκείνου ἀπολύειν. ὑμεῖς δὲ τὸν ἅγιον καὶ δίκαιον ἠρνήσασθε, καὶ ᾐτήσασθε ἄνδρα φονέα χαρισθῆναι ὑμῖν. . . .

ὅτι καὶ κύριον αὐτὸν καὶ χριστὸν ἐποίησεν ὁ θεός,

τοῦτον τὸν Ἰησοῦν ὃν ὑμεῖς ἐσταυρώσατε.

4. A contrast is presented. The hearers killed Jesus when he was among them, but God raised him from the dead. And the speaker and his associate(s) are witnesses to this resurrection.

3:15. τὸν δὲ ἀρχηγὸν τῆς ζωῆς ἀπεκτείνατε,

2:22-24. Ἰησοῦν τὸν Ναζωραῖον, . . . διὰ χειρὸς ἀνόμων προσπήξαντες ἀνείλατε,

ὃν ὁ θεὸς ἤγειρεν ἐκ νεκρῶν,

ὃν ὁ θεὸς ἀνέστησεν λύσας τὰς ὠδῖνας τοῦ θανάτου, καθότι οὐκ ἦν δυνατὸν κρατεῖσθαι αὐτὸν ὑπ᾽ αὐτοῦ.

2:32. τοῦτον τὸν Ἰησοῦν ἀνέστησεν ὁ θεός,

οὗ ἡμεῖς μάρτυρές ἐσμεν.

οὗ πάντες ἡμεῖς ἐσμεν μάρτυρες.

---

differing interpretation of certain elements. Since Schweizer does not develop the comparison it is difficult to criticize his position. See the judgment of Wilckens in note 4. The comparison also differs from the chart appended to Dodd's *Apostolic Preaching*. But on the one hand Dodd does not attempt to give a complete outline; on the other he establishes as an *a priori* that since the first four speeches of Peter cover the same ground they may be taken together to gain a comprehensive view of the content of the early kerygma, a point of view challenged in this chapter.

5. The startling event witnessed by the hearers is linked to Jesus.

3:16. καὶ ἐπὶ τῇ πίστει τοῦ ὀνόμα- τος αὐτοῦ

2:38. ἐπὶ τῷ ὀνόματι ᾿Ιησοῦ Χρισ- τοῦ

τοῦτον, ὃν θεωρεῖτε καὶ οἴδατε,

2:33. τοῦτο ὃ ὑμεῖς καὶ βλέπετε καὶ ἀκούετε.

ἐστερέωσεν τὸ ὄνομα αὐτοῦ, καὶ ἡ πίστις ἡ δι᾿ αὐτοῦ ἔδωκεν αὐτῷ τὴν ὁλοκληρίαν ταύτην ἀπέναντι πάντων ὑμῶν.

2:16-21. ἀλλὰ τοῦτό ἐστιν τὸ εἰρη- μένον διὰ τοῦ προφήτου ᾿Ιωήλ, (citation of Joel 3:1-5a)

6. The hearers and their leaders are excused for their actions due to ignorance. This declaration has no corresponding element in the dis- course of chapter 2.

3:17. καὶ νῦν, ἀδελφοί, οἶδα ὅτι κατὰ ἄγνοιαν ἐπράξατε, ὥσπερ καὶ οἱ ἄρχοντες ὑμῶν.

7. All has been done according to the will of God who foresaw and pre-arranged all.

3:18. ὁ δὲ θεὸς ἃ προκατήγγειλεν διὰ στόματος πάντων τῶν προ- φητῶν, παθεῖν τὸν χριστὸν αὐτοῦ, ἐπλήρωσεν οὕτως.

2:23. τοῦτον τῇ ὡρισμένῃ βουλῇ καὶ προγνώσει τοῦ θεοῦ ἔκδο- τον. . . .

8. The call to repentance is given.

3:19. μετανοήσατε οὖν καὶ ἐπισ- τρέψατε

πρὸς τὸ ἐξαλειφθῆναι ὑμῶν τὰς ἁμαρτίας,

2:38. μετανοήσατε καὶ βαπτισθήτω ἕκαστος ὑμῶν ἐπὶ τῷ ὀνόματι Ιησοῦ Χριστοῦ εἰς ἄφεσιν τῶν ἁμαρτιῶν ὑμῶν, καὶ λήμψεσθε τὴν δωρεὰν τοῦ ἁγίου πνεύματος.

9. Reference is made to Jesus, who is now in heaven, and to his actual relation to the hearers.

3:20-21. ὅπως ἂν ἔλθωσιν καιροὶ ἀναψύξεως ἀπὸ προσώπου τοῦ κυρίου καὶ ἀποστείλῃ τὸν προ- κεχειρισμένον ὑμῖν χριστὸν ᾿Ιησοῦν,

2:33. τῇ δεξιᾷ οὖν τοῦ θεοῦ ὑψω- θεὶς τήν τε ἐπαγγελίαν τοῦ πνεύματος τοῦ ἁγίου λαβὼν παρὰ τοῦ πατρὸς ἐξέχεεν. . . .

ὃν δεῖ οὐρανὸν μὲν δέξασθαι ἄχρι χρόνων ἀποκαταστάσεως πάντων ὧν ἐλάλησεν

2:34-35. οὐ γὰρ Δαυὶδ ἀνέβη εἰς τοὺς οὐρανούς,

λέγει δὲ αὐτός,

21

ὁ θεὸς διὰ στόματος τῶν ἁγίων   (citation of Ps. 110:1=Greek
ἀπ' αἰῶνος αὐτοῦ προφητῶν.   109:1)

10. This element should logically precede #9, for it explains the action of God which has led to the eminent role of Jesus.

3:22-24. Μωϋσῆς μὲν εἶπεν ὅτι προφήτην ὑμῖν ἀναστήσει κύριος ὁ θεὸς ἐκ τῶν ἀδελφῶν ὑμῶν ὡς ἐμέ· αὐτοῦ ἀκούσεσθε κατὰ πάντα ὅσα ἂν λαλήσῃ πρὸς ὑμᾶς. ἔσται δὲ πᾶσα ψυχὴ ἥτις ἐὰν μὴ ἀκούσῃ τοῦ προφήτου ἐκείνου ἐξολεθρευθήσεται ἐκ τοῦ λαοῦ.

καὶ πάντες δὲ οἱ προφῆται ἀπὸ Σαμουὴλ καὶ τῶν καθεξῆς

ὅσοι ἐλάλησαν καὶ κατήγγειλαν τάς ἡμέρας ταύτας.

2:25-28. Δαυὶδ γὰρ λέγει εἰς αὐτόν,
(citation of Ps. 16:8-11=Greek 15:8-11).
2:29-31. ἐξὸν εἰπεῖν μετὰ παρρησίας πρὸς ὑμᾶς περὶ τοῦ πατριάρχου Δαυίδ ὅτι καὶ ἐτελεύτησεν καὶ ἐτάφη καὶ τὸ μνῆμα αὐτοῦ ἔστιν ἐν ἡμῖν ἄχρι τῆς ἡμέρας ταύτης·
προφήτης οὖν ὑπάρχων, καὶ εἰδὼς ὅτι ὅρκῳ ὤμοσεν αὐτῷ ὁ θεὸς ἐκ καρποῦ τῆς ὀσφύος αὐτοῦ καθίσαι ἐπὶ τὸν θρόνον αὐτοῦ, προϊδὼν ἐλάλησεν περὶ τῆς ἀναστάσεως τοῦ Χριστοῦ ὅτι οὔτε ἐγκατελείφθη εἰς ᾅδην οὔτε ἡ σὰρξ αὐτοῦ εἶδεν διαφθοράν.

11. The privileged role of the hearers is pointed out, but it is declared not to be for their benefit alone.

3:25. ὑμεῖς ἐστε οἱ υἱοὶ τῶν προφητῶν καὶ τῆς διαθήκης ἧς ὁ θεὸς διέθετο πρὸς τοὺς πατέρας ὑμῶν, λέγων πρὸς 'Αβραάμ· καὶ ἐν τῷ σπέρματί σου ἐνευλογηθήσονται πᾶσαι αἱ πατριαὶ τῆς γῆς·

2:39. ὑμῖν γὰρ ἐστιν ἡ ἐπαγγελία καὶ τοῖς τέκνοις ὑμῶν

καὶ πᾶσιν τοῖς εἰς μακρὰν ὅσους ἂν προσκαλέσηται κύριος ὁ θεὸς ἡμῶν.

12. A reference is made to the ministry of Jesus and to his preaching of repentance.

3:26. ὑμῖν πρῶτον ἀναστήσας ὁ θεὸς τὸν παῖδα αὐτοῦ ἀπέστειλεν αὐτὸν εὐλογοῦντα ὑμᾶς

2:22. ἄνδρα ἀποδεδειγμένον ἀπὸ τοῦ θεοῦ εἰς ὑμᾶς δυνάμεσι καὶ τέρασι καὶ σημείοις οἷς ἐποίησεν δι' αὐτοῦ ὁ θεὸς ἐν μέσῳ ὑμῶν, καθὼς αὐτοὶ οἴδατε.

ἐν τῷ ἀποστρέφειν ἕκαστον ἀπὸ   2:40. σώθητε ἀπὸ τῆς γενεᾶς τῆς
τῶν πονηριῶν ὑμῶν.   σκολιᾶς ταύτης.

13. This element is not part of the actual discourse, but closely follows
it in each case.

4:4. καὶ ἐγενήθη ἀριθμὸς τῶν ἀν-   2:41. καὶ προσετέθησαν ἐν τῇ
δρῶν ὡς χιλιάδες πέντε.   ἡμέρᾳ ἐκείνῃ ψυχαὶ ὡσεὶ τρι-
                                   σχίλιαι.

Other authors have attempted to explain the similarity between
the discourses in terms of a similar structure. B. Reicke offers the following schema for the "body of Peter's Pentecost sermon":[3]

a. 2:22f. The Jews killed Jesus despite his works.

b. 2:24-31. The scriptures foretold the resurrection.

c. 2:32. The apostles are witness of the resurrection which proves
   that Jesus is the risen Lord.

d. 2:33-35. Through the exalted Christ and his Spirit the wondrous
   events witnessed by the crowd have taken place.

e. Conclusion: Call to repentance.

Reicke has not paid sufficient attention to obvious literary indices
in seeking the structure of the discourse, as will be shown below.
Moreover, in concentrating on the "body" he has chosen to exclude
the Joel citation of 2:17-21 from his structure. Yet this citation is an
integral part of the discourse, as will be shown.

For the moment it is his application of this schema to the discourse
of chapter 3 that is of interest. Using the letters by which the arguments are designated above, Reicke arrives at the following outline:

a. 3:13b-15a.

c. 3:15b.

d. 3:16.

a. 3:17-18. ("Resumption of argument a.")

e. 3:19-20.

b. 3:21-24. ("Additional treatment of argument b.")

e. 3:25-26. ("Resumption of the conclusion.")

He concludes (66-68) by saying that a comparison with the Pentecost sermon reveals a far-reaching agreement in the ordering of the
materials, and that the more evident deviations can be explained by
the peculiar direction of the thought that is observed here. But a
cursory investigation reveals that a similar *ordering* or structuring of

[3] Bo Reicke, *Glaube und Leben der Urgemeinde,* Abhandlungen zur Theologie
des Alten und Neuen Testaments 32 (Zürich: 1957), 44f.

the material is precisely what Luke has *not* presented. It is the material which is similar; it is the ordering which differs.

A more detailed and ambitious analysis was undertaken by E. Schweizer (see n. 2). In the discourse of Acts 2, he noted nine different elements of which four were repeated, or a total of thirteen elements. Of these, eleven are found in the discourse of Acts 3, a striking figure. In the short discourse of 4:9ff., he finds six of the elements, but the next two speeches offer fewer of the elements. Even the longer discourse of chapter 13 exhibits only six of the nine original elements, and these are not in perfect order.

On the basis of this analysis Schweizer argues for a far-reaching identity of structure in the mission discourses of Acts. Wilckens has correctly objected that in this very detailed analysis, schema and individual nuance have not been properly distinguished.[4] The reason lies at hand. Schweizer has attempted to impose a similar structure on speeches which, while they contain many similar elements, differ from one another in the development of thought. What Schweizer has quite convincingly demonstrated is that a striking resemblance exists between the contents of the discourses in Acts 2 and 3, and that this similarity is not present in the other discourses of Acts.

Wilckens approaches the problem from a different point of view. Outlining the contents of the first six mission discourses, he discovers a six-point structure for the discourses of chapters 2, 3, and 13. He does not insist that the structures are identical, but rather that a similar schema underlies all of them (54):

1. All begin by a reference to the situation that has called them forth.
2. The Jesus-kerygma is presented in two parts:
    a. the culpable treatment of Jesus by the Jews
    b. the saving action of God, in which part there is often a proof from scripture for the resurrection or the glorification, as the case may be
3. Finally, there is an announcing of salvation and a call to repentance.

This schema differs only slightly from that offered by Dibelius,[5] and represents an opinion that has steadily gained ground during the past three or four decades so that in one form or another it may be

[4] Wilckens, *Missionsreden,* 54 n. 1.
[5] Dibelius, *Studies,* 165.

safely termed an *opinio communis*. But even with regard to this "minimal" schema certain questions may be raised:

1. The Jesus-Kerygma. The "contrast" presentation of the death and resurrection of Jesus is certainly common to all six of the early mission discourses (2:22-24; 3:13-15; 4:10; 5:30*f.;* 10:39*f.;* 13:27-30; cf. 7:52-56). It represents the peculiar theological viewpoint of the author regarding the salvific value of the acts of Jesus.

2. Announcement of salvation and call to repentance. That salvation is announced in one manner or another in each of the discourses is quite evident. One wonders if a mission discourse would be conceivable without such an announcement. Stephen's discourse does not have such an announcement; but then this is not a mission discourse. But there is no specific *call* to repentance in all of the discourses. In 2:38 and 3:19 there is a direct summons (μετανοήσατε). In 13:40*f.,* the call to accept the remission of sins is negatively stated in the form of a threat. In the speeches of chapters 4 and 5 it is implicit; in the speech of chapter 10 it is completely lacking.

3. Reference to the situation. Each of the first two discourses, as the comparative outline illustrates, begins with a reference to some remarkable event which the onlookers have not grasped; the explanation of the true meaning of the event becomes the starting point of the discourse. In 4:9 Peter begins by referring to the reason why he and John have been summoned before the leaders to defend themselves. Both 5:29 and 10:34*f.* give positive statements of a principle whose application to the situation is developed by the discourse. In the speech of Acts 13, the connection of Paul's opening history of the Jews to the situation is a bit more subtle.[6]

It is true, then, that each discourse responds to the situation in which it is found. But does this warrant the claim that "reference to the situation" is an element in a common schema lying behind the speeches? In Acts 2, the discourse is so closely linked to the Pentecost event in the development of its argument that it cannot be conceived as having been given on some other occasion. But can the same be said for Paul's speech in chapter 13? The speech in itself does not grow out of the situation as does that of chapter 2. "Reference to the situation" is in reality not some precise literary phenomenon, as the peculiar Jesus-kerygma of the speeches is, but the recognition of the fact that Luke has taken pains to make his discourses fit the moment of the story in which they are placed, although in some cases the cor-

[6] *Ibid.,* 166*f.*

25

respondence between discourse and situation is more thoroughgoing than in others.

What then remains of the minimal three-point "schema" proposed by Wilckens? In the end there remains the insight that each of the first six mission discourses contains the same fundamental approach to the Jesus-kerygma, but hardly with some kind of basic schema which can in any way explain the close correspondence in subject matter between the first two speeches of Peter.

Conclusion. Attempts at the isolation of a common structure or a common schema of the mission discourses of Acts do not explain the observable phenomenon of the singular similarity of elements in the first two mission discourses of Peter in Acts.

The Composition of the Mission Discourses

No less striking than the similarity of the speeches of Acts 2 and 3 when analyzed into their component parts is the dissimilarity of the same speeches when the structure given to these parts by the author is studied. A consideration of the other early mission discourses in Acts helps to explain the marked difference between the two speeches.

The Discourse of Acts 2

Concerning the discourse of chapter 2, J. A. T. Robinson has written: "Acts 2 comes to us as the most finished and polished specimen of the apostolic preaching, placed as it were in the shop window of the Jerusalem Church and of Luke's narrative." [7] An analysis of its composition reveals the justice of Robinson's claim:

I. *Structure of the argument.* The discourse obviously divides itself into three parts, each beginning with a salutation (key word ἄνδρες) and concluding with a proof-citation from scripture. A final exhortation is appended as a response to a question of the audience, which question also employs the key word ἄνδρες.

    A. The saluations. There are various formulae of salutation in the addresses of Acts, almost all (notable exception in 4:9) employing the key word ἄνδρες. In the speech of Acts 2, there are three such salutations: The first ἄνδρες 'Ιουδαῖοι (2:14), and the second ἄνδρες 'Ισραηλῖται (2:22), are formal addresses; the

---

[7] "Christology," 185.

third ἄνδρες ἀδελφοί (2:29), is more intimate. The successive salutations show Peter progressively winning over his audience with the result of the mass conversion of 2:41. Thus his auditors reply ἄνδρες ἀδελφοί (2:37), showing that he has achieved rapport. (The same device is used in Paul's first address; see 13:16, 26, 38.)

B. Progression of the argument. The argument is clearly and masterfully presented in the three sections delineated by these salutations:

1. Peter begins by a reference to the wonderful event which has just taken place and which has astounded his hearers. He declares that they are witnessing the eschatological outpouring of the Spirit foretold by the prophet Joel.

2. A new call for attention heralds a fresh start, with at first no apparent connection to what has preceded. The Jesus-kerygma is presented: The Jesus whom you killed has been raised from the dead by God.

3. The third part combines the first two, by showing the relation of the event that has taken place to Jesus. It is itself a brilliant composition. The argument is summed up in 2:36: God has made Jesus both Christ and Lord. Its twofold development proceeds in chiastic fashion:

   a. God has made Jesus messiah by raising him from the dead.
      (a) Ps. 16:8-11 is cited (2:25-28).
      (b) Peter shows that this citation cannot apply to David, for it refers to someone who did not know the corruption of the tomb, whereas David died and was buried, and his tomb is still evident for all to see (2:29).
      (c) Positively, the psalm does apply to Jesus. For David was a prophet, and God had sworn to him that one of his seed would sit on his throne. Thus David spoke this prophecy of the resurrection of the Christ, the messianic Son of David.[8] Since God did raise Jesus from the dead, of which the apostles are witnesses, Jesus is messiah (2:30-32).

   b. God has made Jesus Lord by exalting him to his right hand.
      (c') A positive statement is made about Jesus: Elevated to

[8] The reason for the absence of the title son of David from this speech is discussed by B. van Iersel, "Fils de David et Fils de Dieu," *La Venue de Messie*, Rech Bib 6 (1962), 125.

27

the right hand (or by the power) of the Father[9] and having received from him the promise of the Holy Spirit, he has poured forth this Spirit, thus causing the event to which all the hearers are witnesses (2:33).

(b') A negative statement is made about David: He did not ascend into heaven, which obviously means the citation to follow cannot have him for subject (note adversative δέ) (2:34a).

(a') Ps. 110:1 is cited (2:34a-35). Since Jesus has been elevated by the Father, he is obviously the second κύριος referred to.

It may be objected that perfectly logical construction would demand that the citation of Ps. 16 should follow the third salutation. But Ps. 16:8-11 is concerned with the resurrection, which is also included in the Jesus-kerygma of the second section. Besides, not having punctuation marks at his disposal, Luke needed a means of signaling the end of long and possibly unfamiliar citations of scripture. The means he chose to indicate the close of the two long quotations in this discourse was the introduction of a new vocative.[10] The citation of Ps. 110:1 was too short and well known to need such a device.

II. *Use of scripture.* The manner in which the scriptural passages cited in the speech of Acts 2 have been woven into the texture of the argument suggests that Luke chose them and used them with great care to suit his line of thought.

A. Joel 3:1-5 (Greek 2:28-32a). Certain phrases in the form of the Joel material in Acts 2:17-21, when compared with extant old Greek texts of Joel,[11] suggest that Luke may have adapted his

---

[9] τῇ δεξιᾷ may be either a local or an instrumental dative. Jacques Dupont, "L'interprétation des Psaumes dans les Actes des Apôtres," *Orientalia et Biblica Lovaniensa* 4 (1962), 357-88, argues for the instrumental dative (382-84). Basing himself on the two scriptural citations which introduce and conclude the argument, Wilckens, *Missionsreden,* 152 and nn. 2*f.*, defends the local sense.

[10] Cadbury, "Speeches," 426.

[11] For the textual situation, see *Duodecim Prophetae,* ed. Joseph Ziegler, in *Septuaginta. Vetus Testamentum Graecum auctoritate Societatis Litterarum Gottingensis editum* 13 (Göttingen: Vandenhoeck & Ruprecht, 1943), 235*f.* No known Greek ms (or related version) of Joel 3:1-5 contains the reading, ἐν ταῖς ἐσχάταις ἡμέραις, of Acts 2:17. For the other two readings considered there is support from certain versions, and a few late Greek mss, none of which is dated earlier than the 9th century C.E. Ziegler and others have attempted to explain certain readings found in Greek witnesses to Joel which are in agreement with the

citation to correspond more graphically to the event he was describing.[12]

1. Acts 2:17 begins the quotation with the words καὶ ἔσται ἐν ταῖς ἐσχάταις ἡμέραις λέγει ὁ θεός, where Joel 3:1/2:28 reflects more closely the preserved Hebrew reading ("and it shall be afterwards") through the words καὶ ἔσται μετὰ ταῦτα. The reading found in Acts is not attested by any witnesses to the text of Joel noted in Ziegler's apparatus, and the only texts of Acts to read μετὰ ταῦτα here are codex Vaticanus and the cursive 072—almost certainly an attempt at a "correction" of the text of Acts to agree with Joel.[13]

   a. The meaning of ἐν ταῖς ἐσχάταις ἡμέραις for Luke is that the "last times" are seen as already beginning with the outpouring of the Spirit upon the community.[14] In rabbinic

---

text of Acts 2 as attempts to "correct" Joel by means of Acts. Such a hypothesis is rendered difficult, however, by the fact that none of the witnesses to Joel contains all of the variations of Acts 2. Further, at least one such "correction" appears already in a third century ms (see n. 30). Thus if there were "harmonization," it was both early and sporadic, and not carried through in any known ms or version. In any event, no known version of Joel 3:1-5 in any language contains all three of the special readings from Acts 2:17-21 discussed below.

[12] Eldon Jay Epp, *The Theological Tendency of Codex Bezae Cantabrigiensis in Acts,* Society for New Testament Studies Monograph Series 3 (Cambridge: The University Press, 1966), 66-70, demonstrates the universalistic and anti-Judaic tone of codex Bezae for Acts 2:17 by studying a number of minor variants (which are certainly secondary) not considered here.

[13] The hypothesis that μετὰ ταῦτα was original to Acts is extremely difficult to sustain. James Hardy Ropes, *The Text of Acts, Beginnings* 3, 16, conjectures that ἐν ταῖς ἐσχάταις ἡμέραις is a "Western" reading drawn from ἐν ταῖς ἡμέραις ἐκείναις in Acts 2:18. This latter is then in consistency omitted from D and a few other Western witnesses. Ropes' argument is not impossible, but it is highly improbable that the apparently unmotivated (and mistaken!) substitution would have occurred in the first place, and even more improbable that it should be almost unanimously adopted by admittedly "non-Western" texts. Haenchen's hypothesis is considered in the next note.

[14] In his unpublished dissertation, *Times of Refreshment. A Study of Eschatological Periodization in Judaism and Christianity* (Harvard Divinity School, 1962), William Lane points out that the community regarded the period into which it had entered as "one into which the new age had broken in a proleptic way" (277). Judaism, however, never divides the future age (79), although there was a heightened sense of expectation at Qumran (62). Hence the reading, ἐν ταῖς ἐσχάταις ἡμέραις, is almost certainly the product of Christian exegesis. Ernst Haenchen, "Schriftzitate und Textüberlieferung in der Apostelgeschichte," *ZTK* 51 (1954), 162, argues that since Luke, in opposition to Mark, does not expect an imminent parousia, he is therefore "keineswegs der Meinung, dass mit Pfingsten und der Kirche die Endzeit angebrochen ist." On this basis he regards the reading of codex Vaticanus as original. But it must be objected: (1) Haenchen does not

29

tradition, Joel 3:1 was taken as referring to the final intervention of God in the last times, but the text itself was not
altered as in Acts.[15] Indeed the inventiveness of the Lukan
view lies precisely in his differentiation between the beginning of the last times with the sending of the Spirit upon
those who will be members of the church and their completion with the parousia of Jesus in the distant (but nonethe-
less certain) future. Hence the hypothesis lies at hand that
Luke introduced the words ἐν ταῖς ἐσχάταις ἡμέραις into the
Joel-citation in function of his own view of salvation history.

b. Acts 15:16 presents a difficulty at this point. Luke seems to
be quoting Amos 9:11*f.*, yet the words ἐν τῇ ἡμέρᾳ ἐκείνῃ
introduce this quotation in all known Greek manuscripts
(except two which have the plural)[16] of Amos. In Acts
15:16, on the contrary, all manuscripts read μετὰ ταῦτα. Did
Luke, in speaking again of the time of the church, introduce
the very phrase from which he had departed in Acts 2:17?

Of course there would be no contradiction in such a
procedure, especially since the singular ἐν τῇ ἡμέρᾳ ἐκείνῃ
fits with difficulty into the Lukan scheme. However, a more
satisfactory solution has been proposed by Haenchen and
Cerfaux, namely that Luke was following a special conflation of Amos 9:11*f.* with Jer. 12:15 and Isa. 45:21.[17] Hence
μετὰ ταῦτα is not due to the editorial work of Luke, but to
the source he was using.

In this context it is interesting to note that the Qumran
fragment called 4QFlorilegium contains a quotation of

---

explain why codex Bezae (and Sinaiticus!) should change the supposedly Lukan
eschatology, and the reading of the majority of witnesses remains unexplained.
(2) Since Luke, as is generally agreed since Conzelmann, divides history into three
periods, of which the time of the church is the last, there is no evident reason why
he could not regard the time of the church as the "last times" without retaining
the Jewish notion of an imminent in-breaking of God into history. At least
Haenchen has supplied no such reason. What Luke has done in his work is to
change the traditional notion of the "last times," as Lane has shown.

[15] See *S-B* 2, 615*f.* Joel 3:1 is quoted three times in early rabbinic literature,
each time being introduced by the words *aharei khen* (i.e., μετὰ ταῦτα); Deuteronomy Rabba 6 (203*d*); Targum Joel 3:1-5; Midrash Lamentations 2:4 (65*b*).
There is no evidence for the variants of the Acts text in the rabbinic literature.

[16] According to Ziegler's apparatus two late Greek mss (62, 11th century, and
147, 12th century) read ἐν ταῖς ἡμέραις ἐκείναις for the opening; all other witnesses
have ἐν τῇ ἡμέρῃ ἐκείνῃ.

[17] Haenchen, "Schriftzitate," 164.

Amos 9:11 in an eschatological context, introduced by the expression "in the latter days" (*b'aharit hayyamim*). Moreover, it contains a variant from the masoretic Hebrew of Amos 9:11 that may be due to conflation with other scriptural passages.[18]

Thus it is possible that Luke found the unusual quotation of Amos which he reproduced in Acts 15:16-18 in some kind of collection of sayings concerning the final times. The question may certainly be raised whether the form of the quotation of Joel in Acts 2:17 is not to be explained in the same way.[19]

c. It is not impossible that Luke found the peculiar form of the Joel-citation used in Acts 2:17 in a collection of scriptural passages about the "last days," in which the phraseology of such passages as Isa. 2:2 and Mic. 4:1 was conflated with the citation from Joel. However, if this were true it is surprising that the Lukan variant does not appear in other witnesses to the text of Joel, and it is also surprising that the Joel passage does not seem to have played a sig-

---

[18] The converted perfect form of the verb replaces the imperfect of Amos 9:11. This converted perfect is found two lines above in 4QFlor in a citation of 2 Sam. 7:12. The same form of the quotation of Amos 9:11 is also found in another Qumran document, CD 7:16.

[19] Pierre Prigent, *L'épître de Barnabé I-XVI et ses sources*, Études Bibliques (Paris: Lecoffre, 1961), argues for the use of *testimonia* not only in Irenaeus and Justin, but in Barnabas and the Gospel of Peter. He dates these latter works to the early second century, which would indicate the existence of *testimonia* at the end of the first century. Prigent finds evidence of passion *testimonia* already in the gospel of Mark, and traces the anticultic *testimonia* of Barnabas to certain strains of pre-Christian Judaism. According to Joseph Fitzmyer, " '4Q Testimonia' and the New Testament," *TS* 18 (1957), 513-37, the discovery of 4Q Testimonia at Qumran furnishes "pre-Christian evidence of a literary process that led to the use of composite quotations in the New Testament and thus supports the hypothesis of *testimonia*." Robert A. Kraft, "Barnabas' Isaiah Text and the 'Testimony Book' Hypothesis," *JBL* 79 (1960), 336-50, suggests that Barnabas represents an early stage in the process of "Christianizing" the Jewish practice of using *testimonia*. J. P. Audet, "L'hypothèse des Testimonia," *RB* 70 (1963), 381-405, has pointed out that it is an anachronism to speak of *testimonia* in the sense of published messianic proof-texts in the first two Christian centuries; even at the level of Melito of Sardis and Cyprian one should speak of ἐκλογαί and *excerpta*, which were meant to accompany individual reading. However the practice of making such excerpts was evidently widely known at that period. In addition to the Jewish and Christian examples mentioned above, one need only cite the report of Pliny the younger of his uncle's practice of excerpting for private use (Epistle 3.5). It is a question here, then, of collections of biblical passages made by such excerpting which may have served as a source for Luke's quotations in Acts.

nificant role in early Christian apologetic apart from Acts 2.[20] Thus it remains a possible option that the change in the introductory formula is due to the work of Luke himself.[21]

d. The probability of this option is enhanced by the presence of the words λέγει ὁ θεός,[22] which are not present in any texts of Isa. 2:2, Mic. 4:1 or Joel 3:1/2:28 noted by Ziegler. They might reflect the influence of prophetic utterance forms in general, but the use of θεός rather than κύριος may be taken as a Lukan characteristic for the following reasons: (1) The usual formula in extant old Greek translations of the Hebrew prophets employs κύριος rather than θεός regularly.[23] (2) If Barnabas be taken as an example of an uncreative use of collections of "proof-texts," [24] the use of κύριος is again far more prevalent than θεός.[25] (3) Luke carefully distinguishes θεός (God) and κύριος (Jesus) in this speech.[26]

---

[20] Only Joel 3:5 is cited in Rom. 10:13; there is no reference to the Spirit. Rev. 6:12 seems to allude to Joel 3:4 (ἡ σελήνη ὅλη ἐγένετο ὡς αἷμα). A reference to the Spirit in connection with Joel 3:1-5 is not found until Justin, *Dialogue* 87:6, in conjunction with Ps. 69:19 (cf. Eph. 4:8-10), to show that the power of the Spirit has enabled Christ to bestow gifts upon the faithful—a use which may well depend on Acts. Cf. Barnabas Lindars, *New Testament Apologetic* (London: SCM Press, 1961), pp. 37f.

[21] Dupont, *Sources*, p. 72, concurs with Benoit's conclusion that Luke's method of composition was to work over his own notes. It may be that Luke himself was responsible for the composite quotations in Luke-Acts.

[22] The Western tradition (codex Bezae supported by the Latin and Syriac witnesses) reads κύριος. However a change from θεός to κύριος can be far more easily explained than the reverse, as will be shown in the text and following notes.

[23] The usual form for prophetic oracles is the so-called "messenger form": "Thus saith Yahweh" or "utterance of Yahweh." Thus Otto Eissfeldt, *The Old Testament. An Introduction*, trans. Peter R. Ackroyd (Oxford: Blackwell, 1966), 78f., and Gerhard von Rad, *Old Testament Theology*, trans. D. M. G. Stalker (New York: Harper, 1965), 38f. A cursory reading of the Greek texts indicates the regularity with which this has been rendered by κύριος.

[24] Reference has been made to the studies of Prigent and Kraft above, n. 19. Robert A. Kraft, *Barnabas and the Didache*, The Apostolic Fathers, III (New York: Nelson, 1965), 21, notes "Pseudo-Barnabas' lack of care and/or talent in organizing and editing his materials" in the production of "this well-intentioned but hasty reiteration of school traditions."

[25] While many formulae appear, such as "the prophet says" or "the Scripture (γραφή) says," κύριος (2:5; [3:1] 3:3; 4:8; 6:13, 14, 15; 9:1; 12:1; 16:2; cf. 6:12; 14:3) is the usual way of referring to God as speaker (exceptions: 5:5, 12).

[26] God is referred to as θεός ten times in the speech, and once as πατήρ (2:33). He is referred to as κύριος only in direct quotations of scripture (2:20, 21, 25, 34)

2. Acts 2:18c repeats the words found earlier in 2:17b (Joel 3:1), καὶ προφητεύσουσιν,[27] which underlines the interpretation of the event offered by Luke. The highly complicated textual situation in the old Greek witnesses counsels caution,[28] but the possibility remains that Luke himself has added these words by way of adapting the quotation to the situation.

3. Acts 2:19 contains three words not found in most Greek witnesses to Joel 3:3 (underlined here): καὶ δώσω τέρατα ἐν τῷ οὐρανῷ ἄ ν ω καὶ σ η μ ε ῖ α ἐπὶ τῆς γῆς κ ά τ ω. These words make the citation refer more directly to the event as described by Luke,[29] and, although the textual situation in the old Greek witnesses to Joel is again highly complicated,[30] the possibility must be admitted that Luke himself is responsible for the words indicated. The case is especially strong for τέρατα. While σημεῖα (or the singular σημεῖον) occurs alone four times in Acts (4:16, 22; 8:6, 13), τέρατα occurs only in conjunction with σημεῖα (2:19, 22, 43; 4:30; 5:12; 6:8; 7:36; 14:3; 15:12). Thus the reference to τέρατα in Joel could have inspired Luke to fill out the passage to suit his purposes even more.

The possibility that Luke has adapted the Joel-citation to

---

and once in what will be seen to be a direct allusion to it (2:39). In 2:30 Luke seems to make use of a conflation of Ps. 132:11 (Greek Ps. 131:11) and 2 Sam. 7:12f. The old Greek of Ps. 132:11 begins ὤμοσεν κύριος τῷ Δαυιδ; by contrast, Acts 2:30 has ὤμοσεν αὐτῷ ὁ θεός. On the other hand, Jesus is referred to as κύριος in Acts 2:36, the only occurrence of κύριος outside of scriptural citation and allusion in this speech. Lucien Cerfaux, "Citations scripturaires et tradition textuelle dans le livre des Actes," *Aux sources de la tradition chrétienne. Mélanges offerts à M. Goguel* (Paris: Delachaux and Niestle, 1950), 44, suggests that by dropping the first article from the old Greek of Ps. 110:1 (Greek 109:1) in Acts 2:34, Luke has distinguished God (κύριος) from Jesus (ὁ κύριος) even in this verse. While the observation is attractive, the complicated textual situation both in the old Greek of Ps. 110:1 and in Acts 2:34 precludes a too hasty acceptance of the hypothesis.

[27] Codex Bezae, supported by Old Latin witnesses, does not contain these words. In this case, the omission is probably due to a copyist's error, and the reading of the vast majority of witnesses is to be preferred.

[28] The reading is contained in a few versions, some cursive mss (ninth to fifteenth century), and in Theodore of Mopsuestia according to Ziegler. While the evidence is late, the hypothesis of "harmonization" must not be too hastily accepted, as noted above (n. 11).

[29] In chapter 3 it will be argued that this description is in essence the creation of Luke himself.

[30] One or another of these words is found in numerous mss, versions, or Fathers from the third century onward (e.g., the third century Freer-Washington papyrus), according to Ziegler.

fit the context in which it is used is further encouraged by the observation that the citation forms an integral part of the discourse—it is not simply prefixed to an already existing unity, as contacts with the rest of the speech reveal:

    (1)   In 2:22 the words τέρασι καὶ σημείοις recall the τέρατα καὶ σημεῖα of 2:19.

    (2)   In referring to the event in 2:33, Peter says ἐξέχεεν τοῦτο, using the verb ἐκχεῖν, which is found in 2:17, 18, 33 and nowhere else in Acts.

    (3)   It is possible that τέκνοις in 2:39 is intended to recall υἱοὶ and θυγατέρες of 2:17, and ἐπὶ τῷ ὀνόματι to recall ἐπικαλέσηται τὸ ὄνομα κυρίου of 2:21.

    (4)   The Joel-citation is completed, as it were, in 2:39, by an allusion to Joel 3:5d:[81] ὅσους ἂν προσκαλέσηται κύριος (Joel 3:5d, οὓς κύριος προσκέκληται—the tense change will be considered later).

B.   **Ps. 16:8-11** (Greek 15:8-11). Luke's careful literary composition is also evident in the way in which he has made the citation of Ps. 16 an integral part of the discourse:

    1.   The wording of 2:24 (οὐκ ἦν δυνατὸν κρατεῖσθαι αὐτὸν) prepares us for Ps. 16:10 (οὐκ ἐγκαταλείψεις τὴν ψυχήν). This is especially true if the reading "Hades" of 2:24 (cf. 2:27, 31) is accepted with codex Bezae and other Western authorities.[82]

    2.   Ps. 16:10 is skillfully resumed and paraphrased in the application of 2:31 (ἡ σάρξ αὐτοῦ corresponds to ἡ σάρξ μου of Ps. 16:9).

    3.   After citing the last four verses of the psalm almost verbatim from the Greek scriptures, Luke omits the last stich of the last verse: τερπνότητες ἐν τῇ δεξιᾷ σου εἰς τέλος. The reason is not hard to find: Luke saves the exaltation of Jesus for the second part of the argument, in which he cites Ps. 110:1.

    The citation of Ps. 16 has been skillfully woven into the discourse of chapter 2 and forms an integral and indispensable part of its development. Elsewhere in Acts the psalm is quoted in 13:35, in Paul's Pisidian Antioch speech. Here Acts 13:34-37 gives the impression of being an intrusion into the thought of the discourse, which finds a natural conclusion in 13:38 if

[81] Jacques Dupont, "L'utilisation apologetique de l'Ancien Testament dans les discourse des Actes," *ETL* 29 (1953), 300.

[82] Dupont accepts this reading in the *Bible de Jerusalem*.

this material is omitted. Its purpose would seem to be to explain the relationship between the resurrection of Jesus and his role as Savior: Jesus' immortality is a guarantee of the bestowal of sanctity to the hearers of the word, whereas David, being corruptible, was able to serve only his own generation. But the argument is extremely difficult to follow, and the citations of Isa. 55:3 and Ps. 16:10 would seem to be joined only because of the quite mechanical resemblance of ὅσια and ὅσιον. According to Dupont, it is probable that this line of argument from Isa. 55:3 is to be credited to a source, rather than to Luke himself.[33] It may certainly be claimed that Luke has made a more effective use of Ps. 16 in Acts 2 than in Acts 13, whether or not the achievement is to be attributed to a relative independence from written sources in the composition.

C. **Ps. 110:1** (Greek 109:1). This text is frequently cited in the New Testament relative to the glorification of Jesus. An interesting parallel to its use in Acts 2 is provided by Mark 12:35-37 par., the dispute of Jesus with the scribes, where there is a close connection of the three terms: Christ, son of David, and Lord.[34] In Luke's account Jesus poses a question: How can the Christ be David's son if David calls him Lord (Luke 20:44)? The discourse of Acts 2 gives the answer: Jesus was in truth a descendant of David (2:30), but God has made him both Christ and Lord by raising him from the dead and elevating him to his right hand, as David himself had foretold.

III. *The conclusion.* Luke heightens the dramatic effect by having Peter's discourse end with the summary of 2:36, and by then interjecting a question from the audience who have been cut to the heart by what they have heard:[35] "What are we to do, brothers?" This allows Luke the fullest statement in Acts of what is demanded of one who has been touched by the Christian message:

A. Conversion. The words μετάνοια—μετανοεῖν are found frequently in Luke-Acts, and the call to conversion is essential to

---

[33] Jacques Dupont, "ΤΑ ʿΟΣΙΑ ΔΑΥΙΔ ΤΑ ΠΙΣΤΑ (Acts 13:34=Isa. 55:3)," *RB* 68 (1961), 114 n. 81.

[34] This pericope was probably composed in hellenistic circles. See Ferdinand Hahn, *Christologische Hoheitstitel* (Göttingen: Vandenhoeck and Ruprecht, 1963), 113-15. [English trans. by H. Knight and G. Ogg (London: Lutterworth, 1969).]

[35] Dibelius, *Studies*, 178, calls this an artistic device.

the apostolic preaching according to Luke (cf. Acts 17:30; 26: 20). But the direct appeal, μετανοήσατε, is found in only 2:38 and 3:19.

B. Baptism. Only in this discourse is there an explicit demand that the hearers be baptized. The announcement of the forgiveness of sins is a constant feature of the speeches in Acts, but only here is it linked to baptism.

C. Reception of the Spirit. While the Spirit is mentioned frequently in Acts, only in 2:38 is there a promise in a discourse of the reception of the Spirit as a result of conversion.

The call to conversion in 2:38 is the most solemn and complete of all the discourses. O. Glombitza's analysis of the close of this speech indicates three phenomena which point to its exceptional solemnity: [36]

1. The speech ends with the first "Credo-Formel," namely Ἰησοῦς Χριστὸς Κύριος (2:36). Whereas in in 2:14, 22, 29 the listeners were addressed (ἄνδρες), here we have a solemn proclamation.

2. This credo-formula is not Peter's, but that of all the apostles —2:37 speaks of Peter and the other apostles; 2:42 mentions the διδαχὴ τῶν ἀποστόλων.

3. All the citations in the discourse are given a messianic exegesis so that they can be used as scriptural proofs. This is underlined by the verb διεμαρτύρατο in 2:40. Elsewhere in Acts the verb is used with a subordinate clause; its absolute use here refers to the discourse on the one hand, but also to the emphatic ἑτέροις λόγοις πλείοσιν, which has for content further admonition, proclamation, and promise.

Dibelius calls these last mentioned words (ἑτέροις λόγοις πλείοσιν) a technical device (178). It gives the impression that the speaker actually had much more to say than has been here communicated. Moreover, it leaves the author free to allow the speaker to say only what actually lies in his plan at this point.

IV. *Introduction.* The discourse of chapter 2 is set apart from the other discourses not only by its superb composition, but also by extrinsic indications of Luke.

A. The circumstances of its delivery. The discourse is given on

---

[36] O. Glombitza, "Der Schluss der Petrusrede, Acta 2:36-40. Ein Beitrag zum Problem der Predigten in Acta," *ZNW* 52 (1961), 115-18.

the feast of Pentecost—no other discourse is dated to a feast—before an audience assembled from all over the world.

B. Its collegial nature. While only Peter does the actual speaking, Luke takes pains to indicate that this discourse is to be accredited to the twelve, to the apostolic college which has just (1:26) been reestablished (2:14, 37, 42).

C. The solemn words of introduction:

   1. ἐπῆρεν τὴν φωνὴν αὐτοῦ. In early Christian literature (ἐπ) αἰρεῖν φωνήν is found only in Luke-Acts.[37] In Acts 14:11 and 22:22 it indicates the emotional outcry of a crowd, but in 4:24 it designates the beginning of a solemn prayer of the assembly (cf. Luke 11:27; 17:13). It would seem to have this same function of solemnity in 2:14.

   2. ἀπεφθέγξατο.[38] In the Greek scripture this verb denotes some kind of oracular pronouncement.[39] In early Christian literature its three occurrences are all in Acts: In 2:4 it describes the ecstatic speaking of the apostles after the descent of the Spirit; in 26:25 Paul thus distinguishes what he is doing from the "raving" (μαίνομαι) of which Festus accuses him.

   3. The first call for attention (2:14) employs two parallel members (τοῦτο ὑμῖν γνωστὸν ἔστω/καὶ ἐνωτίσασθε τὰ ῥήματά μου), adding emphasis and solemnity to the opening. Other calls for attention in the discourses employ simply ἀκούσατε, sometimes with, sometimes without an object (2:22; 7:2; 13:16; 15:13; 22:1).

The cumulative force of all these observations supports the judgment of J. A. T. Robinson cited above. It is evident that Luke is in complete control of his material, and has produced a rhetorical masterpiece.

The Other Mission Speeches

A brief consideration of the other mission speeches reveals the singular excellence of the speech of Acts 2. Reserving the speech of

[37] In the Greek scriptures this expression usually occurs in the stereotyped form: Lift up the voice and weep (Judg. 2:4; 21:2; Ruth 1:9, 14; 1 Sam. 11:4; 24:17; 30:4; 2 Sam. 3:32; 13:36). But in Judg. 9:7 it is used to introduce the proclamation of Jotham's fable from Mt. Gerizim.

[38] Alfred Loisy, Les Actes des Apotres (Paris: Emile Nourry, 1920), 196, translates: "Il leur dit oracle."

[39] In four texts in the prophets (Mic. 5:11; Zech. 10:2; Ezek. 13:9, 19) it is used to denote some kind of ecstatic speaking which is looked upon with disapproval. In 1 Chron. 25:1 it has a more favorable meaning, that of prophesying.

Acts 3 for closer scrutiny in the next part, this section studies the addresses of Acts 4, 5, 10 and 13.

I. *Acts 4:8-12.* Peter addresses the sanhedrin.
  A. The point of this brief address is one of considerable importance to the book of Acts, namely the power of the name of Jesus to save. The question that provokes Peter's response already indicates this point: ἐν ποίᾳ δυνάμει ἤ ἐν ποίῳ ὀνόματι ἐποιήσατε τοῦτο ὑμεῖς (4:7) ? Peter restates the question (4:9), and replies that the man was cured in the name of Jesus Christ (4:10), then he goes on to a general statement that salvation is given to men only in this name (4:12).
  B. 4:10 presents in its purest form the consistent Jesus-kerygma of the speeches,[40] with its scriptural justification, namely the oft-cited Ps. 118:22,[41] presented here in a Lukan paraphrase which more clearly parallels the form of the Jesus-kerygma.[42]
  C. This brief address presents succinctly the Lukan notion of the saving action of Jesus, especially as it is expressed in the verb σῴζειν. W. C. van Unnik has noticed that unlike Mark and Matthew, Luke reserves the verb for situations which involve faith; it has a religious connotation at all times.[43] With two exceptions,[44] the same usage is continued in Acts. However, Luke does not ignore the "curative" meaning of σῴζειν. In Luke 8:36, the man possessed by a demon is "saved," i.e., his illness is cured. But he then asks to be a disciple, hinting a more profound, spiritual "cure." Luke similarly employs the ambiguity of σῴζειν in Acts 4:8-12. The leaders ask Peter how a man has been "saved" (σέσωσται). Peter first replies that the man has been healed (παρέστηκεν . . . ὑγιής) in the name of Jesus; but he

---

[40] Wilckens, *Missionsreden*, 44f.

[41] Cf. Lindars, *New Testament Apologetic*, 169-74.

[42] Thus λίθος is modified by two parallel participles, imitating the parallel structure of the Jesus-kerygma of 4:10 (ὅν ὑμεῖς . . . ὅν ὁ θεός . . .) .

[43] See W. C. van Unnik, "L'usage de σῴζειν, 'sauver,' et de ses dérivés dans les évangiles synoptiques," *La formation des Évangiles*, Rech Bib 2 (1957) , 178-94; also Richard Zehnle, "The Salvific Character of Jesus' Death in Lucan Soteriology," *TS* 30 (1969) , 421-23.

[44] Acts 27:20, 31. In the account of the shipwreck διασῴζειν (which never has a religious sense in Luke-Acts) is employed four times (27:43, 44; 28:1, 4) . In using σῴζειν, Luke may be avoiding a too frequent repetition of the same word. However, the symbolic meaning of the shipwreck in Acts must not be excluded. See chap. 3, n. 94. Also compare Acts 27:31 to 1 Pet. 3:20, which refers to Noah's ark which saved only a small group of eight people by water.

goes on to proclaim that only in the name of Jesus are men to be saved (σωθῆναι).

D. The vocabulary of the speech manifests many typically Lukan words and expressions,[45] and nothing suggests dependence on a written source.

Conclusion. All indications point to the free composition of Luke in this brief, but elegant statement of the salvific character of the Jesus-event.

II. *Acts 5:29-32.* Peter again addresses the sanhedrin, this time in the company of all the apostles.

A. The point of Peter's words is complementary to that of the preceding address and fundamental to the apostolic mission, namely that the apostolic preaching is willed and abetted by God. Again the question put to him (5:28) prepares the response by challenging the διδαχή with which the apostles have filled Jerusalem.

B. These verses ostensibly take up expressions from the longer speeches of chapters 2 and 3 (and possibly allude to the speeches of chapters 10 and 13) in summing up and justifying the apostolic kerygma to the Jews.[46]

C. Structurally, Luke has worked out a chiasm which compares the rebellious response to God's initiative on the part of the Jews with the obedience of the apostles:

    (a)   πειθαρχεῖν δεῖ θεῷ (5:29).
    (b)   God raised up Jesus (5:30*a*).
    (c)   Whom you (ὑμεῖς) killed (5:30*b*).
    (d)   Two titles of the exalted Jesus (5:31*a*).
    (d') Two gifts to Israel (5:31*b*).
    (c') We (ἡμεῖς) are witnesses (5:32*a*).
    (b') And the God-given Spirit (5:32*b*).
    (a') τοῖς πειθαρχοῦσιν αὐτῷ (5:32*b*).

D. Luke has bestowed a certain solemnity by making this the response not of Peter alone but of all the apostles (5:29*a*).[47]

---

[45] According to Max Wilcox, *The Semitisms of Acts* (Oxford: Clarendon Press, 1965), 173: "However, examining the passage, we find that it bears a number of marks of the author's style: the six verses 8-13 contain no less than ten Lukanisms [listed in n. 2], while the words οὗτος παρέστηκεν ἐνώπιον ὑμῶν ὑγιής may reflect the kind of use we have in Acts 1:3."

[46] Wilckens, *Missionsreden,* 45.

[47] The facilitating "Western" reading is to be rejected.

Conclusion. Again Luke composes freely, drawing upon his own speeches as "sources" to summarize and justify the apostolic preaching.

III. *Acts 10:34-43.* Peter addresses Cornelius and his companions.

A. This speech differs from the other mission speeches in that it assumes the form of a "history of Jesus." [48] The reason is to be found in the point which Luke is making: The apostles are the witnesses foreordained by God to proclaim the salvation offered through Jesus Christ.

B. The smooth-flowing style of the shorter speeches studied above is notably absent in 10:36-38, the most difficult passage grammatically in all the discourses, if not in all of Acts.[49] The presence of a Semitic substratum which has not been perfectly assimilated into Greek has been argued.[50]

C. The remarkable scriptural exegesis of Acts 2 is missing entirely, and it is difficult to detect a line of argument brought to its logical conclusion in the superb manner of 2:36.

D. Luke's special concerns are not absent from the discourse. 10:39-43 summarizes in four admirably balanced statements the Lukan notion of witness, so essential to the development of Acts.

Conclusion. In the speech of Acts 10, as in the other speeches studied so far, the apologetic concerns of Luke are evident. Yet the elegance, the smooth-flowing argument of the other three speeches is missing, and there is reason to believe that Luke's desire to reproduce more faithfully a written source available to him has somewhat inhibited the rhetorical mastery elsewhere in evidence.

[48] Wilckens, *Missionsreden*, 50: "So scheint die Rede weniger ein Predigt als vielmehr ein Bericht zu sein; man konnte sie von ihrem Hauptteil her am zutreffendsten als '*historia Jesu*' kennzeichnen."

[49] Lake and Cadbury, *Beginnings* 4, 119: "The difficulty of this sentence in the neutral text is (1) absence of connecting particles, which produces a general impression that it is not Greek; (2) the construction of Ἰησοῦν τὸν ἀπὸ Ναζαρέθ which seems to be in a very harsh apposition to ῥῆμα; (3) ἀρξάμενος, which is impossible to construe according to the usual rules of ordinary Greek." J. de Zwann, "The Use of the Greek Language in Acts," *Beginnings* 2, 36, says: "This uneven character of the Greek of Acts must be largely due to the illiterate documents which went into its composition." F. F. Bruce, *The Acts of the Apostles* (London: Tyndale Press, 1951), 225, writes of 10:36*ff*: "The Greek is certainly not Luke's free composition; if it were, it would be much clearer."

[50] Wilcox, *Semitisms*, 116-18. Later Wilcox argues against Torrey's mistranslation theory in favor of the mediate influence of Greek sources (151-53).

IV. *Acts 13:16-41*. Paul addresses the synagogue at Pisidian Antioch.

  A.   The point of this address would seem to be that Paul's listeners must not let the opportunity of salvation pass them by, as the Jews of Jerusalem had already done. Actually what Luke is establishing at this juncture in his story is that Paul proclaims the same message as Peter and the Jerusalem apostles.

  B.   There can be little doubt that Luke has attempted to give this speech a Pauline ring; subtle "Paulinisms" attest to his painstaking work.[51] But the Pauline ending is a surprising conclusion for which the reader has not at all been prepared by the historical summary that opens the speech. Moses, not even mentioned in 13:17-22 (one would expect his name in 13:17 at least), suddenly appears in 13:38*f.* in an unfavorable light, which is singular in Luke-Acts.[52]

  C.   It has been suggested above that the ungainly reference to Ps. 16 is due to a source. Wilcox suggests that Luke is also following "Stephen material" in 13:17-22.[53]

Conclusion. Luke has composed the Pisidian Antioch speech to present Paul and his message as a legitimate continuation of the proclamation of the Jerusalem apostles. Yet the argument lacks the logical development of the speech of Acts 2, and a desire to reproduce written sources may again be the explanation.

The discourses studied so far reveal that Luke has composed each of them for a specific purpose in his overall plan. The technical mastery of his free composition cannot be doubted. Defects in the smooth, logical presentation of the argument seem to be due to a desire to be faithful to written sources.

The Discourse of Acts 3

The discourse of Acts 3, so similar to that of Acts 2 in the elements it contains, is a decidedly inferior piece of literary composition.[54]

---

[51] Cadbury, "Speeches," 411.

[52] The verb δικαιοῦν, which occurs fourteen times in Romans and twice in Galatians, occurs only twice in Acts, in these two verses. Faith is mentioned elsewhere in Acts, but only here is it linked to justification.

[53] Wilcox, *Semitisms*, 21-26; 159-62.

[54] Haenchen, *Apostelgeschichte*, 170: "Sie [the speech of ch. 3] zeigt einen von der Pfingstpredigt recht verschiedenen Stil." Lake and Cadbury, *Beginnings*, 4, 34*f.*: "The construction of almost every sentence in this speech is obscure, and some of it is scarcely translatable, but the general meaning is plain."

I. *Structure of the argument.*

A. General observation. In Acts 2 literary devices (salutations, citations of scripture) set off the three principal divisions which are logically connected so that the third part, chiastically structured itself, ties together the first two. In Acts 3 the progression of thought is not so easy to determine. What precisely, for example, is the role of the glorification of Jesus proclaimed in 3:13? It seems to have no immediate link to the concerns of the hearers as it does in Acts 2.[55] The embarrassment of commentators before the unwieldy progression of this discourse[56] is shown typically in the outline which Reicke has suggested for it, which was reproduced above.

B. Jesus-kerygma. Ordinarily the action of the Jews is presented first (ἀνείλατε 2:23), and that of God follows (ἀνέστησεν 2:24), as in 4:10; 10:39f.; 13:27-30.[57] In Acts 3, Peter begins with the action of God (the singular ἐδόξασεν of 3:13a), then presents the action of the Jews in a somewhat confusing plethora of phrases (13b-15a παρεδώκατε[58]—ἠρνήσασθε—ἠρνήσασθε—[ᾐτή-σασθε]—ἀπεκτείνατε); finally he returns to the action of God in raising Jesus from the dead (ἤγειρεν ἐκ νεκρῶν 3:15b). This is not of course an inadmissible procedure, but the flow of argument is surely less clear and elegant here than in Acts 2.

C. Connection to the situation. Both discourses are occasioned by unusual events which have been misinterpreted by the spectators. In chapter 2, Peter first explains the event in the light of a skillfully adapted Joel-citation, then later shows its meaning in terms of the glorified Jesus (2:33) and the lives of the spectators (2:38). Clearly the event is an essential part of the discourse and works in harmoniously with it. In chapter 3, Peter first states the belief of his hearers with the clear implication that it is

---

[55] 3:26 is no exception. As Haenchen, *Apostelgeschichte*, 169, has noted, ἀνασ-τῆσαι refers to the earthly sending of Jesus, not to his resurrection.

[56] Lake and Cadbury, *Beginnings* 4, 35: "The connection of thought between the first and second parts of the speech is poor."

[57] For 5:30f. the ambiguity of ἤγειρεν comes into play. If it refers to the sending of Jesus by God, then 5:31 introduces the idea of the resurrection, and the order is the same as in the other places mentioned (i.e., "death by Jews—glorification by God").

[58] Haenchen, *Apostelgeschichte*, 165, notes that after ὃν ὑμεῖς μὲν παρεδώκατε "ein entsprechendes δέ und der zum erwartete Satz 'aber Gott hat ihn auferweckt' folgen nicht."

incorrect (3:12b). But he does not illuminate the event by a scripture citation. Moreover the connection to the glorified Jesus is effected by the decidedly ungainly construction of 3:16,[59] and neither the name of Jesus nor faith in the name is connected with the hearers in the call to conversion. Again the flow of argument is less clear than in the discourse of Acts 2.

II. *Use of scripture.*
  A. Acts 3 quotes Deut. 18:15f., 19 (and Lev. 23:29) and Gen. 22:18 to show the relevance of the prophetic message of Jesus, summing them up (ἀναστήσας . . . εὐλογοῦντα) in the final appeal of 3:26. But the carefully worked exegesis of the citations of Acts 2 is lacking.
  B. More significantly, the essential Jesus-kerygma is not proved by specific passages in scripture but by vague general references difficult to substantiate (3:18, 21; cf. 3:24). B. van Iersel [60] defends the hypothesis that the vague general reference to scripture was a feature of the early kerygma; later catechesis added more precise references, so that the general reference itself could be omitted. No such general reference is found in the more polished address of Acts 2.

III. *Conclusion.* 3:19 (and 3:26) calls upon the hearers to accept Jesus' message of repentance, but there is no mention of the Spirit or of baptism, no hint that there is some new community to join. The credo-formula of 2:36 does not appear.

IV. *Setting.* The festal setting of Acts 2, the solemn introduction and the collegial nature of the discourse are all absent from Acts 3.

  Analysis of the composition of the mission discourses indicates that the speech of Acts 2 is the finest specimen of apostolic preaching constructed by Luke, while the speech of Acts 3 is a demonstrably inferior piece of rhetoric. Reference to the discourses of chapters 10 and 13 offers the hypothesis that such inferior workmanship stems from a desire of the author to transmit traditional material he has received.

[59] Lake and Cadbury, *Beginnings* 4, 36 ". . . it is too harsh to be accepted as an ordinary Greek sentence." C. C. Torrey, *The Composition and Date of Acts,* Harvard Theological Studies 1 (Cambridge: Harvard University Press, 1916), has attempted to explain the difficult verse as a mistranslation from an Aramaic original (15f.).

[60] B. van Iersel, *"Der Sohn" in den synoptischen Jesusworten* (Leiden: Brill, 1961), 47-49.

Evidence of Source Material in the Discourse of Chapter 3

Detailed literary analysis reveals the hand of Luke in the composition of the discourse of Acts 3. Nevertheless certain literary phenomena, unusual in Luke-Acts and indeed in early Christian literature as a whole, raise the question of sources used by Luke in the composition of the speech.

Unusual Titles for God

In 3:13 God is named with two titles quite infrequent in early Christian literature in what seems to be a direct allusion to Exod. 3:6.

I. ὁ θεὸς ᾿Αβραὰμ καὶ ᾿Ισαὰκ καὶ ᾿Ιακώβ.[61]

    A.   Mark 12:26 (par. Matt. 22:32). In his discussion with the Sadducees on the question of the resurrection (Mark 12:18-27), Jesus cites Exod. 3:6 in which God declares: "I am the God of Abraham and the God of Isaac and the God of Jacob." Jesus adds: "He is not God of the dead but of the living." F. Dreyfus[62] has demonstrated that at the time of Jesus an expression such as Exod. 3:6 meant that God was the protector of Abraham, Isaac, and Jacob. Thus, the citation is admirably in place in the discussion: God is the protector of Abraham, Isaac, and Jacob; hence they are not dead, but living.

        Luke has clarified and strengthened the argument (20:35-38): Those who have been found worthy to attain to the resurrection are not able to die, but are like angels. This was declared by Moses when he said that the Lord was God of Abraham, Isaac, and Jacob. He is God not of the dead, but of the living, for all live in him.

        Luke's argument has several interesting contacts with 4 Macc.,[63] written perhaps in the same period as Luke-Acts,[64]

---

[61] For the justification of the acceptance of this reading see Wilcox, *Semitisms*, 29f.

[62] F. Dreyfus, "L'argument scripturaire de Jésus en faveur de la résurrection des morts," *RB* 66 (1959), 213-24.

[63] The words πάντες γὰρ αὐτῷ ζῶσιν (Luke 20:38b), proper to the third gospel, find a remarkable parallel in two passages of 4 Macc., both of which also mention Abraham, Isaac, and Jacob: 4 Macc. 7:19 (πιστεύοντες ὅτι θεῷ οὐκ ἀποθνήσκουσιν, ὥσπερ οὐδὲ οἱ πατριάρχαι ἡμῶν ᾿Αβραὰμ καὶ ᾿Ισαὰκ καὶ ᾿Ιακὼβ, ἀλλὰ ζῶσιν τῷ θεῷ); 16:25. Moreover, καταξιωθέντες (Luke 20:35) is the only use of this verb in the third gospel (elsewhere in the New Testament only Acts 5:41; 2 Thess. 1:5); in 4 Macc. it occurs also only once, and in a passage quite similar in meaning to Luke

which systematically emphasizes the belief that those who die for God are not dead, but live in him.[65] This is the same doctrine that Luke records in the story of the rich man and Lazarus (16:19-31) : The patriarchs are not dead, but with God. It is to be noted that although he alters Mark 12:26 [66] Luke nevertheless retains the repetition of θεός before Ἰσαάκ and Ἰακώβ.

B. Acts 7:32. Since the citation of Exod. 3:6 occurs in its historical context in the speech of Stephen, it is difficult to determine the exact sense in which it is to be understood. It is to be noted that in opposition to the reading of most Septuagint witnesses, Acts 7:32 does not repeat θεός before the names of Isaac and Jacob.[67]

C. Acts 3:13. The meaning of the title accepted for Mark 12:26 is particularly suitable for Acts 3:13 where there is question of God's protective action in favor of his servant Jesus. Yet the wording agrees neither with Septuagint nor with Mark 12:26 (cf. Luke 20:37) , but with Acts 7:32.

D. The next explicit mention of the "God of Abraham, Isaac, and Jacob" in Christian literature occurs after the middle of the second century in the writings of Justin. It appears three times in *Apology* 63 (7, 11, 17) in which he contends that the angel that spoke to Moses from the bush was in reality Jesus, the son of God. In each case, θεός is repeated before the names of Isaac and Jacob, as in most Septuagint witnesses. Moreover the words Ἐγώ εἰμι ὁ ὤν are prefixed each time, possibly under the influence of Exod. 3:14.[68]

The formula occurs more frequently in Justin's *Dialogue* indicating a variety of uses at this time.[69] However there is clear reference to a scriptural passage only in 59:2, in which the

---

20:35, namely 4 Macc. 18:3: Ἀνθ' ὧν διὰ τὴν εὐσέβειαν προϊέμενοι τὰ σώματα τοῖς πόνοις ἐκεῖνοι . . . θείας μερίδος κατηξιώθησαν.

[64] Cf. Eissfeldt, *Introduction*, 615.

[65] A. Dupont-Sommer, *Le Quatrième Livre des Machabées*, Bibliothèque de l'école des hautes études (Paris, 1939) , 45f.

[66] Mark 12:26 agrees with LXX in repeating θεός before Ἰσαάκ and Ἰακώβ.

[67] The repetition of (ὁ) θεός in some mss and versions is to be rejected as harmonizing with the Septuagint.

[68] See Wilcox, *Semitisms*, 30. But other possibilities are noted by Joost Smit Sibinga, *The Old Testament Text of Justin Martyr, 1: The Pentateuch* (Leiden: Brill, 1963) , 37f.

[69] See Sibinga, *Text*, 85.

reference is almost certainly to Exod. 3:16. In the other occurrences the wording of the formula varies.[70]

E. According to Hippolytus' *Refutation of All Heresies*, the gnostic Valentinus quoted the following declaration of God to Moses: "I am the God of Abraham, and the God of Isaac, and the God of Jacob; and my name I have not announced to them" (6:31). The reference may be to a special Greek rendition of Exod. 6:2f., since the crucial point in the argument of Valentinus seems to be that God did not announce his name. This use of the title "God of Abraham, Isaac, and Jacob" runs counter to the usage in Acts and Justin, and is probably due to the exegetical effort of Valentinus himself, employing Exod. 6:2f. to bolster his own theological conception.

II. ὁ θεὸς τῶν πατέρων ἡμῶν. While the denomination of God as πατήρ is frequent in early Christian literature, "the God of your (our) Fathers" is found only in the Acts (3:13; 5:30; 7:32; 22:14) in Christian literature before Justin.

A. As indicated in the analysis of the speech of Acts 5, the use of the title in 5:30 probably depends on 3:13.

B. Acts 7:32, as noted above, cites Exod. 3:6 in its historical context. It again differs from the Septuagint which (in agreement with the masoretic text) reads ὁ θεὸς τοῦ πατρός σου. Wilcox finds the plural reading in both Samaritan authorities, the Pentateuch and the Pentateuch Targum, and suggests the existence of a source influenced at some stage by the Samaritan authorities (29f.).

C. Acts 3:13 again agrees with 7:32 against the Septuagint, which suggests that a common source lies behind the two verses.

D. Acts 22:14 poses a special problem. The proximity of this title to other expressions found in the speech in Acts 3 (προχειρίζεσθαι and the title ὁ δίκαιος) suggests literary dependence in one direction or the other. While Acts 22:1-21 probably gives the most primitive form of the narration of Paul's conversion,[71] the varied contacts of Ananias' response to Paul (22:14-16)

---

[70] Thus θεός is not repeated before Isaac and Jacob in 11:1; 35:5; 59:3. In 80:4 it is repeated with the article; in 60:2 and 85:3 it is repeated without the article.

[71] Haenchen, *Apostelgeschichte*, 616-20, shows that Acts 26 has been composed chiefly to express Luke's own theological viewpoint. David Stanley, "Paul's Conversion in Acts: Why the Three Accounts?" *CBQ* 15 (1953), 315-38, regards the speech of chapter 22 as "one of the primary sources" for the account of chapter 9.

indicate that Luke has composed these words, borrowing expressions from other parts of his work to give an archaic ring to the whole.[72] Hence 22:14 probably depends on Acts 3:13 and 7:32, and indirectly on the source behind them.

E. In Justin's *Apology,* chapter 63, the title occurs twice and in the plural (πατέρων) form. However, just as the initial phrase Ἐγώ εἰμι ὁ ὤν may indicate a link to Exod. 3:14, so the plural form may indicate a link to Exod. 3:15 (Septuagint) rather than to a reading of Exod. 3:6 similar to that found in Acts.[73]

Conclusion. The unusual titles for God in 3:13 (and 7:32) may indicate the presence of a special source used by Luke in composing the discourse of Acts 3.

Unusual Titles for Jesus

I. ἀρχηγὸς τῆς ζωῆς (3:15). The title ἀρχηγός for Jesus is extremely rare in early Christian literature. It occurs only in Acts 3:15; 5:31 (the latter in dependence on the former); Heb. 2:10; 12:2; and 2 Clem. 20:5. W. Grundmann sees this title as coming from the hellenistic circle; it betrays the influence of the "Heracles myth" and implies the use of the Septuagint.[74] But A. Descamps judges hellenistic parallels of the title hardly conclusive; he argues instead that the source of the title is the Septuagint, and in particular the terminology used for Moses.[75]

In fact, as will be demonstrated later, there is an extended Moses-Jesus parallel in the discourses of Acts 3 and 7. The latter address cites Exod. 2:14 to the effect that Moses is ἄρχων and δικαστής; both titles are paralleled for Jesus in Acts 3. The use of ἀρχηγός instead of ἄρχων for Jesus is probably explained by a

---

[72] ἔσεσθέ μου μάρτυρες recalls the final command of Jesus to the apostles in Acts 1:8. ἐπικαλεσάμενος τὸ ὄνομα αὐτοῦ recalls Acts 2:21 and with the mention of baptism and the remission of sins that precedes it presents the programmatic call to conversion of 2:38. But τί μέλλεις, good classical Greek, is the only occurrence in the New Testament of the absolute use of the verb in the sense of "delay." The middle, βάπτισαι, occurs only here in Acts. Hence Acts 22:14-16 is probably a Lukan composition, but employing words and concepts from earlier parts of his work.

[73] See Wilcox, *Semitisms,* 30. However, as Sibinga, *Text,* p. 38, points out, the matter is somewhat more complicated since Justin reads the singular of the pronoun (σου) as in Acts 7:32, whereas the other places in Acts read ἡμῶν.

[74] W. Grundmann, "Das Problem des hellenistischen Christentums innerhalb der jerusalemer Urgemeinde," *ZNW* 38 (1939), 45-73, especially 65-70.

[75] A. Descamps, *Les justes et la justice dans les évangiles et le christianisme primitif* (Louvain: Gembloux, 1950), 65-71.

desire to indicate the difference between Jesus and Moses,[76] or perhaps to avoid equivocation between Jesus and the chiefs of the people, often designated as the ἄρχοντες in Acts (as in 3:17).

Bruce has pointed out[77] that ἀρχηγὸς τῆς ζωῆς is equivalent to the ἀρχηγὸς τῆς σωτηρίας of Heb. 2:10, since ḥayyê in Aramaic can signify either "life" or "salvation." [78] It is quite possible, then, that the title of Acts 3:15 is an alternate rendering from an Aramaic original of the same title found in Heb. 2:10, a title not destined to be widely used in the community.

II. παῖς (3:13, 26). Except in quotations[79] and prayers[80] the title παῖς[81] is used of Jesus very rarely in early Christian literature. Its occurrence in Barn. 6:1 [82] in a form of Isa. 50:8f. known otherwise only in two texts of Irenaeus (*Apostolic Preaching* 88; *Against Heresies* 4.33.13) suggests its presence in a book of *testimonia*, but if so, surprisingly little use is made of it.[83] In the Epistle to Diognetus 8:9, 11 and 9:1, παῖς is used to designate Jesus as the pre-existent *son* of God, and similar uses are found in later writers.[84] These uses bear little resemblance to Acts 3:13, 26, which emerges as a rather singular passage in the literature.

The fact that παῖς as a title for Jesus is found in the prayer of the Jerusalem community in Acts 4:27, 30, and in liturgical prayers of the Didache (9:2b, 3; 10:2f.), suggests its archaic character, since liturgy tends to conserve older traditions. J. Jeremias has argued for an Aramaic origin of the title.[85] It seems to have been

---

[76] As δικαστής for Moses, δίκαιος for Jesus; λυτρωτής (7:35) for Moses, σωτήρ (5:31) for Jesus.

[77] Bruce, *The Acts of the Apostles*, 109.

[78] Haenchen, *Apostelgeschichte*, 166, n. 5, sees a liturgical formula behind 3:14, Heb. 2:10, and 2 Clem. 20:5 (σωτῆρα καὶ ἀρχηγὸν τῆς ἀφθαρσίας).

[79] Matt. 12:18 quotes Isa. 42:1; Barn. 9:2 contains what is probably a quotation from Isa. 50:10a in an anthology (9:1-4a) calling men to "hear." See Kraft, *Barnabas*, 106.

[80] Acts 4:27, 30; Did. 9:2b, 3; 10:2f.; Mart. Pol. 14:1, 3; 20:2; 1 Clem. 59:2-4; Acts of Paul and Thecla 24.

[81] The other words which translate 'ebed in the Greek scriptures need not be considered here: θεράπων is not used of Jesus in early Christian literature, and δοῦλος is found of Jesus only in Phil. 2:7, in a context greatly different from the παῖς-sayings under consideration.

[82] Prigent, *Barnabé*, 169-71; Kraft, *Barnabas*, 95.

[83] Kraft, "Barnabas' Isaiah Text," 346.

[84] Thus Hippolytus, *Treatise on Christ and Antichrist* 3; Clement of Alexandria, *The Rich Man's Salvation* 34.

[85] J. Jeremias, *The Servant of God*, SBT 20, 2nd rev. ed. (1965), 81-84.

largely avoided as a title in hellenistic circles, either because the connotation of "servant" made it unacceptable as a popular designation of Jesus, or because "it did not seem to bring out the full significance of the majesty of the glorified Lord." [86]

Passages within the early Christian prayers mentioned above suggest an origin of the title for Jesus in Davidic typology.[87] However, after a survey of the relevant literature, Jeremias concludes that "the description of David as 'servant of God' is to be found solely in prayers" (50). Hence the use of the title in Acts 3:13, 26 may be due to another influence. Moreover, Haenchen approves the suggestion of Dibelius that Luke himself introduced παῖς into the prayer of Acts 4 in dependence on Acts 3:13.[88]

While παῖς is attested as a title for many of the great figures of Jewish history, it seems to have a wide usage only for Moses.[89] Hence it is possible that, while the early prayer material may reflect David typology, the use of παῖς for Jesus in Acts 3:13, 26 is due to Moses typology.

III. ὁ ἅγιος καὶ δίκαιος (3:14). This compound title, found nowhere else for Jesus in early Christian literature,[90] stands in marked contrast to the compound κύριος καὶ χριστός of Acts 2:36, which is decidedly Lukan (see below). Each element of the title must be considered separately.

A. ὁ δίκαιος. The "just (one)" was an epithet of great honor in both Greek and Jewish literature.[91] While the Just One is not widely attested as a title for Jesus, it is predicated of him in several different ways, which must be considered here.

---

[86] *Ibid.*, 86. Cf. C. Maurer, "Knecht Gottes und Sohn Gottes im Passionsbericht des Markusevangeliums," *ZTK* 50 (1953), 38.

[87] Acts 4:25 speaks of Δαυὶδ παιδός σου; Did. 9:2a of Δαυὶδ τοῦ παιδός σου.

[88] Haenchen, *Apostelgeschichte*, 186.

[89] According to Jeremias, *Servant*, 50: "This title of honor is firmly established only for Moses," though it is used of David, Noah, Abraham, and others. The name of Jeremiah might be added to the list in the light of the *Paralipomena Jeremiae*. See Gerhard Delling, *Jüdische Lehre und Frömmigkeit in den Paralipomena Jeremiae* (Berlin: Töpelmann, 1967), 19f.

[90] Mark 6:20 refers to John Baptist as ἄνδρα δίκαιον καὶ ἅγιον which may be fortuitous, but which at least indicates that Mark did not understand the compound as a peculiar title for Jesus. In a passage of the Letter to Diognetus (9:2) Jesus is referred to as ὁ υἱός, ὁ ἅγιος, ὁ ἄκακος, ὁ δίκαιος, ὁ ἄφθαρτος, and ὁ ἀθάνατος.

[91] Gottlob Schrenk, "δίκαιος," *TDNT* 2, 182-91.

According to Matt. 27:19, Pilate's wife advises him to have nothing to do with τῷ δικαίῳ ἐκείνῳ. Here as in Luke 23:47 (and Matt. 27:24 if the variant reading be accepted) the evident meaning is that Jesus is innocent of the crime of which he is accused. Whether the evangelist is alluding to a (messianic) title for Jesus on a deeper level must remain an open question.

Barn. 6:7 refers to Jesus as the Just One in what appears to be a citation of Isa. 3:9b-10a. The author seems to be utilizing traditional proof-texts in this section, and this particular text has been traced from Wis. 2:12 to such Christian writers as Justin (*Dialogue* 16:4f., 17:3, 119:3, 133-37), Tertullian (*Against Marcion* 3:22) and Clement of Alexandria (*Stromata* 5.108.2).[92] Isa. 57:1 is often combined with Isa. 3:9b-10a, suggesting the servant of Yahweh who suffers unjustly at the hands of sinners.

The notion of expiatory suffering is stressed in 1 Pet. 3:18 which declares that Jesus died for sins, δίκαιος ὑπὲρ ἀδίκων. In a similar vein 1 John 2:1f. declares that Jesus is a just advocate with the Father and is the expiation for the sins of the world.[93]

Basic to each of these conceptions is the innocence of Jesus in the face of his persecutors. Wilckens argues that a similar meaning underlies both δίκαιος and ἅγιος in Acts 3:14. They are to be understood in a moral sense, in contrast to the ἀνὴρ φονεύς.[94] Thus the compound title would simply underline the innocence of Jesus over against the culpable action of the Jews.

While it is true that Luke takes pains to underline the innocence of Jesus in his two-volume work, the moral sense of δίκαιος does not seem to explain its titular use in Acts 3:14. In the first place, it is not evident that the compound title is meant to be contrasted to ἀνὴρ φονεύς, as Wilckens claims. The ἀρχηγὸς τῆς ζωῆς would seem to be a more natural counterpart to the murderer.[95] Secondly while δίκαιος may possibly have the

[92] Kraft, *Barnabas,* 96; Prigent, *Barnabé,* 178-82.

[93] See also *Epistle to Diognetus* 9:5 and Clement of Alexandria, *The Instructor* 1:6 (in which Jesus' blood is said to intercede before God as Abel's did).

[94] Wilckens, *Missionsreden,* 170. Similarly H. Dechent, "Der 'Gerechte'—eine Bezeichnung für den Messias," *Theologische Studien und Kritiken* 100 (1927/1928), 439-43, argues that δίκαιος for Jesus denotes moral purity and nobility.

[95] G. Macgregor, *The Acts of the Apostles,* The Interpreter's Bible 9 (Nashville: Abingdon Press, 1954), 58.

moral sense, when used by itself, it is here coupled with ἅγιος which cannot be construed as implying the innocent sufferer (see below).

Descamps has argued that Moses typology—already seen as a possibility for the two previous titles—stands behind the designation of Jesus as ὁ δίκαιος.[96] When Moses is called "the Just" in the rabbinic literature, it is not in the sense of the innocent and passive Abel; it is as leader of his people. Descamps concludes: "The typology of Moses and of the servant of Yahweh suggest that ὁ δίκαιος should be understood as a title of honor, reserved for a prophet, and indicating his powerful role" (78).

B. ὁ ἅγιος. Jesus is entitled ὁ ἅγιος only in Mark 1:24 (par. Luke 4:34), in the mouth of a demon; John 6:69, by Peter; Rev. 3:7; and Acts 3:14. Its use as a title for Jesus was evidently not widespread.[97]

According to O. Procksch [98] there is nothing in the Old Testament that would prepare the use of the Holy One as an epithet for the messiah. Rev. 3:7 does not offer an explanation of why the title should be applied to Jesus. Mark 1:24 seems to reflect the theology of the evangelist, as the Holy One of God is set over against the πνεῦμα ἀκάθαρτον of 1:23.[99]

Once again a source may be suggested for the title in Moses typology. In Wis. 11:1 Moses is referred to as προφήτης ἅγιος; all the prophets are qualified as holy in Luke 1:70; Acts 3:21. In John 6:69 Peter confesses that Jesus is ὁ ἅγιος τοῦ θεοῦ. The context is remarkable. Chapter 6 opens with the multiplication of the loaves by Jesus, and the crowd exclaims: οὗτός ἐστιν ἀληθῶς ὁ προφήτης ὁ ἐρχόμενος εἰς τὸν κόσμον (6:14); moreover they try to make Jesus their king (6:15). Later there is a discourse on the bread of life which is filled with a Moses-Jesus contrast regarding the manna that Moses gave to the fathers in the desert. Thus, the whole chapter attests the combination of con-

---

[96] Descamps, *Les justes*, 76-79.

[97] Jesus is referred to as the "holy servant" in Acts 4:27, but this may be due to Luke (see n. 88). In Acts 2:27 and 13:35 Jesus is called ὁ ὅσιος. But this is a quotation from Ps. 16:10 (Greek 15:10), and the title is not found of Jesus elsewhere. Even the adjective ὅσιος is found only rarely in early Christian literature. See F. Hauck, "ὅσιος," *TDNT* 5, 489-92.

[98] O. Procksch, "ἅγιος," *TDNT* 1, 88-97.

[99] See James M. Robinson, *The Problem of History in Mark*, SBT 21 (1957), 35f.

cepts: Moses-type, prophet, holy. Jesus, the prophet like Moses, is holy because of his prophetic consecration.

Thus the compound title, ὁ ἅγιος καὶ δίκαιος, does not refer only to the innocence and moral uprightness of Jesus. It is a messianic epithet of the prophet like Moses.

Conclusion. The speech of Acts 3 contains several titles for Jesus which do not seem to have been popular designations in the hellenistic community. In each case there is some possibility that the use of the title for Jesus is connected to Moses typology.

It may be objected that the speech of Acts 2 contains an early title for Jesus not contained in the speech of Acts 3, namely 'Iησοῦς ὁ Ναζωραῖος (2:22). It must be admitted either that archaic titles for Jesus indicate nothing about the primitive character of the material in which they are found, or that chapter 2 along with chapter 3 contains a discourse embodying considerably older material.

In the first place it is not at all certain that ὁ Ναζωραῖος was an early title for Jesus. The similar form, Ναζαρηνός, found consistently in Mark [100] and twice in Luke[101] may well be an early designation of Jesus as one coming from Nazareth. But Ναζωραῖος[102] cannot satisfactorily be derived etymologically from the place name "Nazareth." The most convincing explanations of the origin of the title are those which see Ναζωραῖοι as a designation of the members of the community independently of their connection to Jesus. B. Gärtner[103] suggests that the new community, which regarded itself as the eschatological remnant of Israel, adopted the designation *niṣurim* (those preserved: Isa. 49:6), which can be rendered Ναζωραῖοι in Greek. M. Black[104] suggests that Ναζωραῖοι, from its similarity to a self-designation of the Mandaean sect, originally designated the followers of John Baptist, and that its use for Christians arose "through their popular identification" with them. The application of the title ὁ Ναζωραῖος to Jesus would then be a later derivation from an early name for the community, probably at a time when the origin was no longer known

[100] Mark 1:24; 10:47; 14:67; 16:6.

[101] Luke 4:34 (Mark 1:24); 24:19 (possibly influenced by Mark 16:6). Cf. 18:37 D *et al.*

[102] Matt. 2:23; 26:71; Luke 18:37; cf. 24:19 D *et al;* John 18:5, 7; 19:19; Acts 2:22; 3:6; 4:10; 6:14; 22:8; 26:9. Also Acts 9:5 and 26:16 vars. cf. 24:5.

[103] B. Gärtner, *Die rätselhaften Termini Nazoräer und Iskariot,* Horae Soederblomianae 4 (Uppsala: C. W. K. Gleerup, 1957), 14-18.

[104] M. Black, *An Aramaic Approach to the Gospels and Acts,* 3rd ed. (Oxford: Clarendon Press, 1967), 197-200.

and Ναζωραῖος was regarded as the equivalent of Ναζαρηνός (Matt. 1:23).

The title occurs six times for Jesus in Acts, and once for the community (24:5). Luke undoubtedly found it in his sources, but its frequent use may be said to be typical of him, to the point that the direct influence of a source may be questioned each time the title occurs. Its use in 2:22 is undoubtedly an attempt by Luke to give an archaic ring to the Pentecost discourse, just as he has done for the discourses of chapters 4 and 26, again discourses which are undoubtedly his original compositions. It is perhaps significant to note that in introducing this archaic element into the event recounted in chapter 3, he has chosen to mention it explicitly only in the healing narrative (3:6), which betrays the hand of Luke in every verse, while simply alluding to Jesus' "name" in the discourse itself (3:16).

Unusual Titles for the Audience

In Acts 3:25 Peter addresses his hearers with two titles that are unique designations of the Jews in the New Testament:

I. υἱοὶ τῶν προφητῶν. To appeal to the Jews as "Sons of the Prophets" is not only to use a title found nowhere else in early Christianity; it assumes an attitude which must be deemed singular in the literature, especially when taken in conjunction with the reference to the hearers as being sons of Abraham in the second part of the passage. In Matt. 23:31 Jesus berates the scribes and Pharisees as being the sons of those who killed the prophets (υἱοί ἐστε τῶν φονευσάντων τοὺς προφήτας). Luke 11:47 is a parallel to the "woe" of Matt. 23:29-31, but there is in Luke no reference to the "sons of those who killed the prophets." For the notion of the Jews as "sons of Abraham," there are certainly other attitudes in the New Testament:

A. John 8:39-44. When the Jews claim to be children of Abraham, Jesus replies: "If you are children of Abraham, do the works of Abraham." He argues that since they do not behave as Abraham did, they cannot be called his sons. Neither are they sons of God, but sons of the devil.

B. Gal. 2:7 (cf. Rom. 4; 9:6-8). Paul tells the Galatians that it is those who have faith who are the sons of Abraham.[105]

[105] 2 Cor. 11:21f. is only an apparent exception to Paul's consistent attitude in Gal. and Rom. His "boasting" is part of an *ad hominem* argument and does not mean

C. Matt. 3:9; Luke 3:8. To the Jews who refuse to repent, trusting in their physical descent from Abraham, John Baptist replies: "God can raise up from these stones children to Abraham."

D. Luke 19:9. A more favorable attitude to the notion of descent from Abraham is evidenced in the comment of Jesus: "Today salvation has come to this house, in as much as he also is a son of Abraham." Yet being a son of Abraham does not seem to save if there is no conversion, as the parable of the rich man and Lazarus shows (Luke 16:19-31).

It would seem that in a more developed Christian awareness, especially after the definitive break with the synagogue, physical descent from Abraham was played down considerably in favor of the spiritual descent of faith. Luke was quite aware of this stage of thinking but in this early discourse of Acts he has preserved a more primitive and more open stance on the part of the new community.[106] Peter flatters his hearers by recalling their prerogatives to them.

II. υἱοὶ . . . τῆς διαθήκης. Early Christianity was forced to come to grips with a fact insisted upon by the writings it regarded as scripture, namely that God had made a covenant with Israel.

A. Paul's writings contain a deep ambivalence. On the one hand salvation was something new in Christ, the fulfillment of the promise made to Abraham (Gal. 3; Rom. 4). The Law was a temporary dispensation (Gal. 3:19, 23-25); in fact it had become a curse since no one could observe it fully (Gal. 3:10), a curse from which Jesus redeemed mankind (Gal. 3:13f.). On the other hand, Israel's election was real, and its effects, at least inasmuch as God's relation to the Jews is concerned, were lasting (Rom. 9:6; 10:1-4; 11). Thus Paul could draw examples from the experience of Israel for the instruction of the faithful,

---

that he considers physical descendance from Abraham as a thing to boast of in itself. See Dieter Georgi, *Die Gegner des Paulus im 2. Korintherbrief,* WMANT 11 (1964), 63-82.

[106] Paul's use of "sons of Abraham" (υἱοὶ γένους 'Αβραάμ) in 13:26 is in the same spirit. The Jews of Jerusalem seem to reject the apostles decisively in chapter 12, but in chapter 13 Paul is addressing Jews outside the Holy Land. He explicitly distinguishes them from the inhabitants of Jerusalem who were responsible for the death of Jesus (13:27ff.). By using the title "sons of Abraham" in a laudatory way he is offering them the same freedom of choice which the Jews of Jerusalem had, but to which they responded so poorly.

for just as Israel was elected by God, so was the church elected to receive the salvation effected in the death and resurrection of Jesus Christ.

But such claims leave a question to be answered: If the Law was a temporary dispensation incapable of giving salvation, then what further place has Judaism in God's plan? How can a temporary covenant still stand in any sense if the time has been fulfilled? Did Israel have a real meaning in its own right in the history of salvation or did it not?

B. One direction taken by later Christian thinkers was to play down the reality of the Jewish dispensation, to deprive it of any value other than the symbolic. Thus, the author of the epistle to the Hebrews sees Israel as merely a shadow of the reality of the new covenant. The phrase of 8:5, ὑποδείγματι καὶ σκιᾷ, which should be translated as a hendiadys, "obscure image," [107] underlies the scriptural exegesis of chapter 9 in which the regulations for worship are seen as a foreshadowing of the sacrifice of Jesus. The word διαθήκη is used more in Hebrews than in any other early Christian work, yet the author never says in so many words that God made a covenant with the Jews.[108] He insists on the new covenant of which Jesus is the mediator, and on the importance of the promise to Abraham. The superiority of the Christian dispensation receives far more attention than any notion of its continuity with Judaism.

The Epistle of Barnabas goes further. The Jews rejected the covenant with God at Sinai; hence it cannot be said that the covenant ever belonged to them, but only to the Christians (4:6-8; 13-14).

C. The mainstream of Christian thought, however, took a different direction. The covenant between God and Israel had been a real one, but now Christianity had taken the place formerly occupied by Judaism in God's plan. Thus Christians could claim the Jewish scriptures as their own.[109] Luke-Acts belongs in this stream of thought, as will be shown in the next chapter.

[107] Ceslaus Spicq, *L'Epître aux Hébreux,* Études Bibliques 2 (Paris: Gabalda, 1953) , *ad loc.*

[108] This is of course implied in the term "first covenant" (9:15), but never specifically stated by the author. The term "old covenant," which might tend to stress continuity rather than superiority, is avoided.

[109] See I Clem. 29:1-30:1 and 64:1 in which it is evident that the community is regarded as having replaced Israel as God's chosen portion. Cf. Eph. 2:12, 19*f.*; 1 Tim. 1:6-11; 4:13; 2 Tim. 3:16*f.*

D. It is not surprising, then, that to call a Jewish audience "sons of the covenant" in an evidently complimentary manner is singular in early Christian literature.[110] The notion of διαθήκη does not play an extensive role in Luke-Acts.[111] Hence it is altogether probable that Luke is depending on some source for the use of this title.

Conclusion. In Acts 3 there are titles used to refer to the audience in a complimentary way, which later received uncomplimentary connotations as Christianity developed and began to regard itself as a rival to Judaism.

Non-Lukan Terminology

Here there is not a question simply of vocabulary, but of terms used to designate definite theological concepts:

I. *Forgiveness terminology.* In place of the usual Lukan ἄφεσις ἁμαρτιῶν (cf. 2:38) the speech of Acts 3 employs expressions found nowhere else in Luke-Acts:

A. ἐξαλειφθῆναι (3:19). Aside from the quotation of Ps. 51 (50 in the Greek Psalter) in 1 Clem. 18:2, 9, the verb ἐξαλείφειν is used only here and in 2 Clem. 13:1 in early Christian literature to signify the remission of sins.[112] In Greek Jewish scriptures the verb is used frequently to designate the blotting out of sin or injustice,[113] but none of the passages offers a clear literary contact with Acts 3:19. It is significant that only in this passage of Acts is the verb ἐπιστρέφειν in the sense of moral conversion not followed by a prepositional phrase denoting the object to which one is to convert.[114]

---

[110] Only Rom. 9:4 is in the same spirit, though the larger context (Rom. 9–11) is not. Commenting on the importance of the notion of covenant in Judaism W. D. Davies, *Paul and Rabbinic Judaism* (London: SPCK, 1948), 261, cites a prayer "that probably goes back to the first century" which acknowledges God's mercy towards "the sons of Thy covenant" (Tos. Berg. 3.7).

[111] It occurs only in Luke 1:72 (the Benedictus, for which Luke has certainly used sources); 22:20 (the manuscript evidence is divided; if the reading is original, then it has been taken over from the liturgy); Acts 3:25; 7:8 (which records a fact in the history of Israel).

[112] The literal sense of the verb (to blot out, to wipe away, to erase) occurs in Rev. 3:5; 7:17; 21:43; Herm. 101. (Sim. 9.24) 4; 1 Clem. 53:3-5. Col. 2:14 (ἐξαλείψας τὸ καθ' ἡμῶν χειρόγραφον) is similar in meaning.

[113] Ps. 51:1, 11; 108:14 (ἁμαρτία); Sir. 40:12; 41:11; 46:20; Isa. 43:25; Jer. 18:23 (ἁμαρτίας); 2 Macc. 12:42.

[114] The usual expression is ἐπὶ τὸν κύριον (9:35; 11:21) or ἐπὶ (τὸν) θεόν (14:15;

B. ἐν τῷ ἀποστρέφειν ἕκαστον ἀπὸ τῶν πονηριῶν ὑμῶν (3:26). The use of ἀποστρέφειν to refer to the conversion of others from evil is unique in early Christian literature. Its only other use in Luke-Acts is in Luke 23:14 when Jesus is referred to as "misleading" the people. Similarly, the plural of πονηρία is used nowhere else in Luke-Acts in the sense of "sins," and rarely in this sense in early Christian literature.[115]

II. *End-time terminology.* Acts 3:20*f.* refers to the end time with two terms found nowhere else in the New Testament:

A. καιροὶ ἀναψύξεως. The word ἀνάψυξις is a New Testament ἅπαξ.[116] In the Septuagint it is found only in Exod. 8:11 where it translates the Hebrew *rewaḥa* which refers to the relief from one of the plagues of Egypt. It is tempting to see a parallel in Isa. 32:15 where Symmachus reads ἀνάψυξις ἐξ ὕψους in place of the old Greek (ἕως ἂν ἐπέλθῃ ἐφ᾽ ὑμᾶς) πνεῦμα ἀφ᾽ ὑψηλοῦ. Luke cannot have known Symmachus' translation, if, as is usually held, it was not produced before the late second century;[117] a similar Greek version of Isa. 32:15 may have existed earlier, but this must remain a conjecture.[118]

15:19; 26:20); it is used once with εἰς φῶς (26:18). 28:27 is a citation of Isaiah, and the other uses (9:40; 15:36; 16:18) are in the physical sense of "turning to."

[115] Aside from the citation of Isa. 1:16 in 1 Clem. 8:4, only Herm. 15. (Vis. 3.7) 2 and 38. (Man. 8) 3 are clear examples. Herm. 14. (Vis. 3.6) 3 probably refers to the plurality of persons involved; cf. W. F. Arndt and F. W. Gingrich, *A Greek-English Lexicon of the New Testament and Other Early Christian Literature:* a translation and adaptation of W. Bauer's *Griechisch-Deutsches Wörterbuch* . . . (Chicago: University Press, 1957), *sub voce.*

[116] Luke 21:36 contains the related verb ἀποψύχειν, also in an apocalyptic connection.

[117] Theodotion reads ἄνεμος ἐξ ὕψους which would seem a more justifiable translation of the Hebrew (*rûaḥ mimmārôm*) than that of Symmachus. It is probable that Theodotion's translation antedates Luke: Cf. D. Barthélemy, *Les devanciers d'Aquila,* Supplements to Vetus Testamentum 10 (Leiden: Brill, 1963), 148.

[118] Lane, *Times of Refreshment,* 169-72, holds that the influence of the text of Symmachus can be seen in the "Western" tradition, which he reconstructs as follows: ὅπως ἂν ἐπέλθωσιν (D, h) ὑμῖν (E, e, h, Iren, Tert, Syr[hl], Arm, Vg[codd]) καιροὶ ἀναψύξεως. Although both of the variant readings are found only in h (and Tertullian), this Latin text is perhaps the most important single text in determining the Western readings in Acts. See James Hardy Ropes, *The Text of Acts, Beginnings* 3, cviii, and Epp, *Tendency,* 29. However, according to the report of Theodore C. Petersen, "An Early Coptic Manuscript of Acts: An Unrevised Version of the Ancient So-called Western Text," *CBQ* 26 (1964), 225-41, the Coptic text G[67], which may be "the earliest completely preserved and entirely unadulterated" witness to the Western text (226), contains neither of the readings under con-

W. Lane finds a Semitic counterpart to καιροὶ ἀναψύξεως in the rabbinic *qorat ruaḥ,* i.e., "the cooling of the spirit." This phrase is included in a description of the eschatological times in Aboth 4:17, which is to be attributed to Rabbi Jacob ben Kurshai (160–222 A.D.) .[119]

According to F. Preisigke[120] ἀνάψυξις refers to the repose of the souls of the dead in heaven. He cites a tombstone inscription which reads: ἐν τόπῳ φωτινῷ, ἐν τόπῳ ἀναψύξεως. The translation "refreshment" seems justified, and the expression "times of refreshment" is probably a reference to the paradisiacal situation hoped for in the new eon in apocalyptic speculation.[121] But neither the word nor the concept plays a further role in Acts.

B. χρόνων ἀποκαταστάσεως. The word ἀποκατάστασις is used only here in the New Testament. However it recalls the verb ἀποκαθιστάναι which is associated in the New Testament with the restoration to be effected by Elijah.[122] Matt. 17:11 and Mark 9:12 echo this tradition, but the reference is omitted in Luke, who in general avoids the Elijah-John Baptist parallel.[123] The only occurrence of the verb in Acts is in 1:6, the disciples' question about restoring the kingdom to Israel.[124] The use of the related noun in 3:21 may reflect the same thought milieu.

---

sideration. Thus it must remain problematical whether Lane's restoration gives the original "Western" reading, and whether the "Western" reading is the original.

[119] *Ibid.,* 172-75.

[120] F. Preisigke, *Wörterbuch der griechischen Papyruskunden* 1 (Berlin: Selbstverlag der Erben, 1925) 113.

[121] F. Mussner, "Die Idee der Apokatastasis in der Apostelgeschichte," *Lex Tua Veritas: Festschrift für H. Junker* (Trier: Paulinus-Verlag, 1961), 293. Lane, *Times of Refreshment,* 178-80, contends that a temporal distinction must be made between καιροὶ ἀναψύξεως (the outpouring of the Spirit, already experienced by the community at Pentecost, but still to be experienced by Peter's hearers), and the χρόνοι ἀποκαταστάσεως (the consummation, the days of the messiah, which are still to come). Such a distinction, which is not the obvious sense of the Greek text, is based upon the understanding of ἀνάψυξις which has been questioned above, and upon Lane's thesis that the Jerusalem community quickly came to a new conception of periodization of the eschatological times (as already begun, but not yet consummated). Little evidence can be found to support the conjecture, for which a detailed criticism is beyond the scope of this note.

[122] Mal. 3:23f. foretells the sending of Elijah which will precede the day of the Lord: καὶ ἰδοὺ ἐγὼ ἀποστέλλω ὑμῖν Ἠλίαν . . . ὃς ἀποκαταστήσει καρδίαν. . . .

[123] Conzelmann, *Theology,* 22-26.

[124] Wilckens, *Missionsreden,* 155, has noted a literary contact between Acts 1:6 and Sir. 48:10d: καὶ καταστῆσαι φυλὰς ’Ιακώβ. Sir. 48:1-11 refers to Elijah.

Noting these peculiarities, Bauernfeind[125] holds that it is not credible that Luke has forged 3:20*f.*, a kind of statement so foreign to him and to the entire New Testament, as a mere stylistic variation to 1:7. But for an author who so evidently makes use of sources as Luke does, there is always the possibility that, finding it impossible to restate a source in his own style, he will adopt that of the source itself. Naturally such a piece of tradition acquires a certain importance.

Bauernfeind maintains that the original milieu of these lines was a "baptist community," a group of disciples of John Baptist. Little change would be needed to take them over; besides, the link with the Messiah-Jesus instead of Elijah had already been made. The ease with which the modulation from the Baptist key to the Christian was made pointed in Luke's judgment to the generation which had received the message of both the Baptist and Jesus, namely the early apostolic time.

That Acts 3 assigns to Jesus an Elijah-like function seems evident enough. But the conjecture of a baptist community is as unnecessary as it is unfounded. Jesus was probably regarded by some during his lifetime as the Elijah who was to come (Mark 6:15). Later reasoning about the place of John Baptist in relation to Jesus assigned him the role of Elijah, but as forerunner of Jesus, not of the eschatological times. Since he seems to have rejected this development, Luke would have no difficulty employing a tradition which ascribed an Elijah-function to Jesus.[126]

Conclusion. The appearance of several technical terms in the discourse of Acts 3, evidently not those commonly employed by the author of Luke-Acts, points to the existence of a source on which he depended in constructing the discourse.

Literary analysis then reveals considerable evidence of material in the discourse of Acts 3 which seems to indicate that Luke was relying on sources that may be quite primitive.[127] O'Neill has objected to

---

[125] O. Bauernfeind, "Tradition und Komposition in den Apokatastasisspruch. Apg. 3:20*f.*," *Abraham Unser Vater: Festschrift für O. Michel* (Leiden: Brill, 1963), 13-23.

[126] See P. Dabeck, "Siehe, es erschienen Moses und Elias," *Biblica* 23 (1942), 175-89.

[127] Marked similarities between the discourse of Acts 3 and the Benedictus (Luke 1:68-79) in concepts (God's intervention connected to a covenant-Fathers-Abraham concatenation of ideas; the mission of a prophet in terms taken from the Elijah-

commentators who conclude from the "conjunction of unusual Christological terms around chapters 3, 4, and 5 of Acts" that they have "suddenly struck a rich vein of early Christology." His own conclusion is: "Chapters 3, 4, and 5 provide an exuberance of uncommon titles because Luke is striving to give an archaic and scriptural ring to that part of Acts where a final appeal is made to the Jews in Jerusalem to accept their Messiah." [128] The same objection may be extended to all the material considered in this section: Luke is deliberately archaicizing; there is no need to assume primitive sources.

To this it must be replied: First, Luke has somehow come into contact with some relatively unfamiliar titles and terms which he knew would give an archaic flavor to the discourse of Acts 3 and the surrounding material. Second, he has chosen to reproduce this material precisely in the discourse of Acts 3, and not that of Acts 2—and to a far lesser extent in the short addresses of Acts 4 and 5. Hence it would seem possible that Luke also might have had access to primitive christological notions, and that he would reproduce these precisely in that discourse in which he has used archaic titles and terminology. The next chapter will take up the question of thought content in greater detail.

Conclusion

Literary comparison reveals a far-reaching similarity between the discourses of Acts 2 and 3 in the elements of which they are composed, a similarity which cannot be explained by a hypothesis of common structure or common schema. Yet the discourse of Acts 2 is evidently the finest mission discourse composed by Luke, while that of Acts 3 is decidedly inferior. The presence of seemingly primitive titles and technical terms not characteristic of Luke-Acts in the speech of Acts 3 suggests the hypothesis that Luke was strongly dependent on early source material in its composition.

---

tradition of Mal. 3) and even in wording (cf. Acts 3:21 and Luke 1:70) naturally raise the question of dependence. There is little doubt that Luke used sources in composing the Benedictus. Cf. Pierre Benoit, "L'enfance de Jean Baptiste selon Luc 1," *NTS* 3 (1956/1957), 169-94; J. Gnilka, "Der Hymnus des Zacharias," *Biblische Zeitschrift* 6 (1962), 215-38. But simple dependence of Acts 3 on the Benedictus is precluded by two instances in which the discourse contains non-Lukan expressions where the hymn has typically Lukan ones: (1) For the remission of sins, the Benedictus has ἐν ἀφέσει ἁμαρτιῶν (1:77), while Acts 3:19 has εἰς τὸ ἐξαλειφθῆναι ὑμῶν τὰς ἁμαρτίας; (2) The visitation of God in the Benedictus will bring σωτηρία (1:69, 71, 77), but in Acts 3:20 the καιροὶ ἀναψύξεως are awaited.

[128] O'Neill, *Theology*, 145.

2. The Speeches and the Thought Content of Luke-Acts

The speeches of Acts 2 and 3 both purport to be addresses given by Peter in the first days of the Jerusalem community, preaching conversion and salvation to the Jews. This chapter investigates the thought content of the two discourses in the light of the total theological viewpoint of Luke-Acts, to discover whether there are elements in them that may properly be called non-Lukan, i.e., elements which derive directly from sources that may shed some light on a relatively early stage of Christian reflection.

Acts 2: An Epitome of Lukan Theology

Luke puts into the mouth of Peter on Pentecost a brief statement of the theological perspectives developed in his two volume work.

Salvation

The mission discourses typify the work of the community, the announcement of salvation to the world. In Luke 24:47 the risen Jesus hinted at the future work of the apostles when he said that in his name μετάνοια and ἄφεσις ἁμαρτιῶν would be preached to all nations. The call to conversion runs throughout Acts—it is demanded of Jew (2:38; 3:19; 5:31) and Gentile (17:30); after baptizing the first pagan, Peter declares to the church at Jerusalem that God has given to the Gentiles also μετάνοιαν εἰς ζωήν (11:18); and Paul, in summing up his ministry to the Ephesian elders, insists that he has proclaimed τὴν εἰς θεὸν μετάνοιαν (20:21; cf. 26:20). The remission of sins is seen as the effect of conversion (2:38; 5:31; 10:43; 13:38; 26:18). But in Acts a positive thrust is given to the call to conversion by the inclusion of elements first mentioned in the Pentecost discourse:[1]

---

[1] Conzelmann, *Theology,* maintains that μετάνοια loses its comprehensive meaning in Luke-Acts. The process by which a person is saved can be divided into "repentance" and "conversion"; thus there are works which follow upon repentance

1. *Jesus, and faith in his name.* According to Peter, the remarkable event witnessed by his audience was the eschatological outpouring of the Spirit upon the disciples by Jesus, who is now exalted in heaven as Christ and Lord (2:33). Hence, whoever wishes to be saved (2:41*b*) must receive this Spirit by being baptized in the name of Jesus (2:38), a clear reference to the final verse of the Joel-citation that opened the discourse (2:21) —"Whoever calls upon the name of the Lord will be saved" (Joel 3:5).

The short discourse of Acts 4:8-12 declares that in the name of Jesus and in no other is salvation given to men. Thus Peter proclaims that all the prophets bore witness to the fact that through the name of Jesus everyone who believed in him would receive the remission of sins (10:43).

When the Philippian jailer asks Paul and Silas: "Sirs, what must I do that I may be saved?" they reply simply: "Believe in the Lord Jesus, and you will be saved and your whole household" (16:30*f*.). Hence, in the summation of his ministry before the Ephesian elders cited above, Paul also states that he has borne witness to Jews and Greeks of πίστιν εἰς τὸν κύριον ἡμῶν ʾΙησοῦν (20:21).

In Acts, salvation is not connected directly to the death of Jesus on the cross in the sense that he is said to have died for our sins.[2] But inasmuch as he has been glorified and empowered to send the Spirit, Jesus does have an active role in the salvation of those who believe in him.[3]

2. *The Spirit.* As noted above, the conversion demanded by Peter of his hearers will result in their reception of the Spirit (2:38), which is necessary if they wish to be saved from their crooked generation (2:41*b*).

The Spirit plays a most important role in Luke's presentation of salvation. Already in the Jewish Scriptures the Spirit is depicted as speaking through the prophets and inspired writers;[4] explicit reference is made to the fulfillment of what was spoken by the Spirit in certain

---

which must now be considered separately (99-101). In the same direction, see R. Michiels, "La conception lucanienne de la conversion," *ETL* 41 (1965), 42-78.

[2] Wilckens, *Missionsreden*, 216*f.;* Conzelmann, *Theology*, 201; Haenchen, *Apostelgeschichte*, 82.

[3] Wilckens, *Missionsreden*, 185: While the reception of salvation is usually eschatological-futuristic in the rest of the New Testament kerygma, it is present according to Luke in the name and person of Jesus. Cf. Zehnle, "Salvific Character," 425-32.

[4] W. Barnes Tatum, "The Epoch of Israel: Luke I-II and the Theological Plan of Luke-Acts," *NTS* 13 (1966/1967), 187*f.*

key incidents in Acts (1:16; 4:25; 28:25). But this spirit of prophecy, which is also to be met within the infancy narrative,[5] was something temporary. In the life of Jesus something new appears, the permanent gift of the Spirit, so that Jesus may justly be called Lord of the Spirit.[6]

At the time of his baptism, Jesus is filled with the Spirit (Luke 3:22; 4:1) and in this power he undertakes his mission (4:14), a fact alluded to in his first words (4:18, 21). Only Luke records Jesus' rejoicing in the Spirit (10:21) in his declaration of his privileged knowledge of the Father. The commission to the apostles (Acts 1:2) is given through the Holy Spirit, and Peter tells Cornelius and his companions that the ministry of Jesus was accomplished under the guidance of the Spirit (10:38).

During the lifetime of Jesus "the Spirit rests upon one person only." [7] But after Jesus' ascension and exaltation the Spirit is given to every believer at the time of his conversion (Acts 2:38; 9:17; 15:8), or at least at the time of his full reception into the community (8:17; 19:6). This possession of the Spirit is permanent; those selected by the apostles to be "deacons" are said to be full of the Spirit (6:3).

3. *The community.* But faith in the name of Jesus and the reception of the Spirit do not give a total picture of the conversion necessary for salvation. Peter calls upon his hearers to perform a public act, that of baptism (2:38). Their separation from the crooked generation (2:41*b*) is not merely an internal decision; it is ratified by a rite, an initiation ceremony. Hence Luke concludes his narrative: "On that day about 3,000 souls were *added*" (2:41). They joined the new community.

The community is regarded from the beginning of Acts as the *locus* of the saved (2:44, 47). Hence Peter insists on baptism for Cornelius and his companions, even though they have already received the Spirit (10:47).[8] True conversion necessarily implies becoming a member of the new community through baptism.[9]

The clearest indication of the role of the community in salvation is given by Luke's use of the term λαός. In the infancy narrative the

[5] For John Baptist (1:15, 80*a*); Elizabeth (1:14); Zechariah (1:67); Simeon (2:25-27).

[6] Tatum, "Epoch," 190.

[7] Conzelmann, *Theology*, 184.

[8] *Ibid.*, 208.

[9] Michiels, "Conversion," insists on the ecclesial nature of repentance in Acts.

word occurs eight times; in the gospel itself there are 29 uses, of which 27 are peculiar to Luke and seem to be additions of the author.[10]

The infancy narrative introduces the first theme: The angel tells Zechariah that John Baptist will prepare a λαός for the Lord (1:17), an idea resumed by Zechariah in the Benedictus (1:68). In 2:10 the birth of Jesus is said to be a cause for great joy among the λαός. The Canticle of Simeon prepares for a future development: In 2:31 the word is used in the plural, and 2:32 mentions the revelation to the Gentiles.

In the gospel John Baptist's mission to the λαός is briefly described (3:15, 18); all the people accept his baptism (3:21; 7:29). They are likewise the recipients of the mission of Jesus; in Luke Jesus comes down from the mountain to give the sermon on the plain, which is heard by a great multitude of the λαός (6:17; 7:1). In 19:47 the people are distinguished from their leaders (πρῶτοι); the λαός hears Jesus willingly, but the leaders wish to kill him and are prevented only by their fear of the people.[11]

But an evil fate awaits this people (21:23). In Luke the λαός is clearly implicated in the death of Jesus, though not so severely as in Matthew. Jesus is accused of stirring up the people (23:5, 14), and the λαός is called upon to witness his innocence along with the chief priests and leaders (23:13).[12] The entire group calls for his death. A multitude of the λαός follows Jesus to Calvary to watch him die (23:

[10] In Mark λαός occurs only twice: Once in a citation (7:6), and in 14:2 when the leaders fear to arrest Jesus because of the possibility of a tumult among the people. Matthew uses it 14 times, but only two uses are significant: 1:21, when the angel declares that the child "will save his people from their sins"; and 27:25, where the people condemn Jesus and call his blood down upon themselves. Elsewhere it occurs mostly as a genitive qualifier or in citations. Matthew's use of λαός in 1:21; 27:25 only suggests the importance that the word might have; there is no systemization of its use.

[11] Luke 20:6; 20:19, 26; 22:2 of the triple tradition in which the fear of the people is more strongly expressed in Luke.

[12] According to G. Rau, "Das Volk in der lukanischen Passionsgeschichte; eine Konjektur zu Luke 23:13," ZNW 56 (1965), 41-51, the reference to the λαός in Luke 23:13 so contradicts the Lukan tendency to accentuate the difference in attitude between the people and their leaders (as opposed to Mark, where the difference gradually disappears) that it is necessary to conjecture an original ἄρχοντας τοῦ λαοῦ which a scribe would have changed to ἄρχοντας καὶ τὸν λαόν by inadvertence. The conjecture lacks any ms support; hence to be convincing it must be demanded by the totality of Luke-Acts. Yet Peter clearly states that his listeners are guilty of the death of Jesus in the discourses of Acts 2 and 3, and in Acts 3 he is addressing the λαός (3:12). Hence, the conjecture is to be rejected.

27, 35). The leaders blaspheme, but the crowds are remorseful, seeing what has happened.

The history of the λαός is continued in Acts (48 occurrences). In the beginning the Jewish people are favorable to the apostolic preaching (2:47; 5:13), and glorify God for what is happening, thus preventing the leaders from harming the apostles (4:21; 5:26). They still have the opportunity to repent and accept the salvation offered by Jesus since they are repeatedly designated as the object of the apostolic preaching and teaching,[13] and indeed seem favorably disposed.

But in 6:12, the λαός is stirred up against Stephen. In 12:3f. Herod sees that they are pleased with the death of James, and tries to kill Peter. But the latter escapes from τοῦ λαοῦ τῶν Ἰουδαίων (12:11); the qualified title indicates the beginning of a change. In his speech at Pisidian Antioch, Paul addresses the λαός (13:15), and reviews God's dealings with the Jews from the exodus (13:17) to the mission of John Baptist (13:24). The inhabitants of Jerusalem and their leaders rejected Jesus, but after his resurrection those who had accompanied him from Galilee were witnesses of him to the λαός (13:31). Paul then announces salvation to this part of the people which is outside of Jerusalem, and many follow him (13:43). But the greater part do not, and as a group stir up opposition to the apostolate of Paul (13:45, 50). Previously in Acts, οἱ Ἰουδαῖοι had an unfavorable sense only in the attempt to kill Paul (9:23) and in the people's pleasure at the death of James (12:3). Now that the diaspora Jews have joined the Jews of Jerusalem in rejecting the message of salvation, οἱ Ἰουδαῖοι becomes a *terminus technicus* (as in the fourth gospel) for the opponents of Paul, the bringer of salvation.[14]

However James (brother of the Lord) interprets Peter to the effect that God has chosen a λαός from among the Gentiles (15:14). In 18:10 Paul is told in a vision that God has a great λαός predestined in the city (Corinth); it is largely made up of non-Jews. There is now a new λαός.[15]

And the chosen people? Chapter 21 shows their hatred for Paul, whom they accuse of preaching against their people. Before Agrippa Paul explains why the Jews persecute him, but trusts God to deliver him from the people (26:17). Finally in 28:17ff., after his last unsuc-

[13] Acts 3:9, 11, 12; 4:1, 2, 10, 17, 21; 5:12; 6:8.
[14] Acts 14:2, 4; 17:5, 13; 18:12; 20:3, 19 *etc.*
[15] N. A. Dahl, "'A People for his Name' (Acts 15:14)," *NTS* 4 (1957/1958), 319-27, disagrees. But see Epp, *Tendency*, 76f., for a refutation of his argument.

cessful confrontation with the Jews, Paul pronounces the terrible prophecy of Isaiah against the λαός—and on this note, the Acts closes.

Summing up, the author of Luke-Acts has presented an outline of the history of salvation in his use of the word λαός:

a. The λαός, the chosen people Israel, was the recipient of the good news proclaimed by Jesus.

b. The λαός responded favorably to Jesus, but their leaders plotted against his life, and the people joined them in having him put to death.

c. Yet the door of salvation was still open to the λαός, and many accepted the apostolic preaching.

d. From the Jews who accepted the gospel and from the Gentiles, God chose a new λαός. The Jews who refused the gospel were rejected.

Thus a community of believers in Acts is the new people of God to whom salvation has been given. Whoever wishes to be saved must join himself to this community by a profession of faith in Jesus Christ, signified by baptism in his name.

Conclusion. The discourse of Acts 2 presents in a nutshell the Lukan notion of what it means to be saved that is maintained consistently throughout the book: The hearers must repent and make a profession of faith in the name of Jesus (by baptism); then they will receive the Holy Spirit and enter the community of the saved.

Christ and Lord

Against these arguments for the Lukan thought content of the discourse, it has been asserted that the christology of the speech embodies a view which is manifestly not that of Luke, that Luke has reproduced an earlier christology which is not his own. J. A. T. Robinson maintains that Acts 2:36 contradicts the point of view of the third gospel, where "the application of 'Christ' and 'Lord' is pushed back, not merely behind the Resurrection, but behind the Baptism, to the birth of Jesus." [16] According to F. Hahn,[17] an "adoptionistic" statement as Acts 2:36 is genuinely Jewish and scarcely conceivable in hellenistic Gentile Christianity.

It is not, however, a question of what Luke, the Gentile Christian could or could not have done; it is a question of what he did. Acts 2:36 makes a statement about the two most meaningful christological titles

[16] "Christology," 180.
[17] Hahn, *Hoheitstitel,* 117.

in Luke-Acts;[18] investigation of these two titles in his work must decide whether or not the christology of Acts 2:36 contradicts the overall view.

I. κύριος. C. F. D. Moule[19] has shown that Luke's use of κύριος, far from being indiscriminate, carefully reflects the unfolding of events in the third gospel and Acts. In the narrative sections of the gospel, it is true, Luke more than the other evangelists refers to Jesus as the Lord.[20] But other than the vocative κύριε, which "as a common form of address hardly holds the same possibilities as κύριος," [21] the title is restricted on the lips of men to three cases: 1:43, 76; 19:31. (Angels are of course allowed to use it, 2:11.) In 1:76 the reference to Jesus (as κύριος) is only one of the possible interpretations, and a Christian one at that; the ambiguous κύριος for God or Jesus occurs frequently only in Acts. Elizabeth's greeting to Mary (1:43) is inspired prophecy, and 19:31, 34 is the phrase of Jesus himself. As a general rule, then, Luke does not write back into the life of Jesus a title which seems to be postresurrectional in his view. But already in Luke 24:34 the situation had changed, and Cadbury's remark is correct, that κύριος Ἰησοῦς (Χριστός) was considered by Luke "as the appropriate way to speak of him within the Christian circle. Certainly for use within that circle Luke has no other term for Jesus except the simple form ὁ κύριος." [22] Moule notes "three particularly striking phenomena" in Acts: the strangely absolute phrase of Peter to Cornelius in 10:36 (οὗτός ἐστιν πάντων κύριος) ; the interchange of κύριος for God or Jesus, especially in Old Testament testimonia; and the phrase ἐπικαλεῖσθαι τὸ ὄνομα "which, undoubtedly used in certain instances with reference to the name of Jesus, is irresistibly reminiscent of the Old Testament idea of invoking the name of Yahweh (cf. Acts 2:21 with 7:59; 9:14, 21; 22:16) and implies the invocation of the divine." [23]

Thus Luke's use of κύριος in 2:36 to proclaim that by the resur-

[18] O'Neill, Theology, 119.

[19] C. F. D. Moule, "The Christology of Acts," Studies in Luke-Acts, 160f.

[20] H. Cadbury, "The Titles of Jesus in Acts," Beginnings 5, 359: Matthew 0; Mark 0; John 5; Luke 13.

[21] Moule, "Christology," 160. Hahn, Hoheitstitel, 74-95, argues for the use of the mar-title in the lifetime of Jesus. But this is convincingly refuted by P. Vielhauer, "Ein Weg der neutestamentlichen Theologie? Prüfung der Thesen F. Hahns," EvT 25 (1965) , 24-72.

[22] Cadbury, "Titles," 360.

[23] Moule, "Christology," 161.

rection God had made Jesus Lord is in complete harmony with the general usage of Luke-Acts, and explains what Luke evidently regards as the most important and most current title of Jesus.

II. χριστός. According to Cadbury, "The result of the evidence in Acts concerning χριστός is certainly to compel us to acknowledge that for this writer it is not a proper name." [24] He offers a series of arguments:

A. χριστός is used fourteen times in Acts as a title.
B. In several instances in Luke-Acts it is used for the Old Testament messiah without special reference to Jesus (Luke 2:26; 3:15; 24:26, 46; Acts 2:31).
C. In Acts 2:36 it is used in the predicate.
D. Luke evidently understands the etymology from his use of χρίειν in Acts 4:27 (cf. Luke 4:18; Acts 10:38).
E. The combination "Jesus Christ" has only limited use in Acts. Of its eleven uses, seven occur with τὸ ὄνομα and are evidently a formula. Similarly in 9:34 and 10:36 "Jesus Christ is spoken of as the agent of cure or of the message of good news." In the other two cases (11:17; 15:26) there is question of the full credal formula: κύριος 'Ιησοῦς χριστός.
F. Alone among New Testament passages, Luke 2:26 "reproduces the accurate idiom which requires the possessive κυρίου with χριστός." [25]

Cadbury's conclusion is that this is quite possibly a successful attempt at archaism. It is certain that Jesus Christ had become almost a proper name at the time of Luke's writing;[26] his insistence on χριστός as a title is undoubtedly a conscious attempt to explain the second of the two most important names for Jesus.

Robinson's objection, that Luke has pushed the title back to the birth of Jesus, which then makes Acts 2:36 a contradiction, presents no real difficulty when it is seen that, for Luke, to be the Christ necessarily meant to suffer and thus to enter into glory (Luke 24:26). Jesus was the Christ at birth, but he still had to become the Christ by performing the messianic role foreordained by God.[27] It is not that

---

[24] Cadbury, "Titles," 358.
[25] Cf. the citation of Ps. 2 in Acts 4:26.
[26] According to Werner Kramer, *Christ, Lord, Son of God*, trans. Brian Hardy, *SBT* 50 (1966), 203-14 (#60-65), the only passage in the Pauline corpus in which it is relatively certain that χριστός is a title (and not a name) is Rom. 9:5.
[27] Luke insists that the entire life of Jesus was a conformity to the preordained

Jesus was messiah-designate at one moment and actually the messiah at another; rather, different moments represent stages in his being the messiah.

III. *Composition of Acts 2:36.* While the notions behind the statement of Acts 2:36 are certainly pre-Lukan, the statement itself and its place in the development of Luke-Acts are probably due to the work of Luke himself.

A. That Jesus became the Christ through the resurrection was probably a conclusion drawn by the Jerusalem community itself. From an analysis of the earliest credal statements in the Pauline letters, W. Kramer concludes that the Aramaic-speaking church found the basis for the messianic status of Jesus in the notion that God had raised him from the dead. Hence its basic credal statement was that God raised *Jesus* from the dead. The pre-Pauline hellenistic church then substituted *Christ* for Jesus when the resurrection-statement was combined with a passion-statement.[28]

To say that God made Jesus "Christ" by raising him from the dead would then most likely be a formulation of the Aramaic-speaking community.

B. But the notion of κύριος in Acts 2:36 is manifestly not the *mar*-title of the Aramaic-speaking church.[29] It is the hellenistic community's conception of Jesus as Lord which, as noted above, had become the most widespread title for Jesus at the time of Luke. Thus to say that God made Jesus Lord by raising him from the dead is probably the formulation of the hellenistic community.[30]

---

role of the messiah by his use of δεῖ and πορεύεσθαι. Cf. W. Grundmann, "δεῖ," *TDNT* 2, 22*f.*; E. Fascher, "Theologische Beobachtungen zu δεῖ," *Neutestamentliche Studien für R. Bultmann,* ZNW Beiheft 21 (1954), 246; U. Luck, "Kerygma, Tradition und Geschichte Jesu bei Lukas," *ZTK* 57 (1960), 63; F. Hauck and S. Schulz, "πορεύομαι," *TDNT* 6, 574; W. C. Robinson, *Der Weg des Herrn,* Theologische Forschung 36 (Hamburg: Herbert Reich, 1964), 39-43.

[28] Kramer, *Christ,* 42 (#8*e*).

[29] The *mar*-title was adopted for Jesus precisely because it was "relatively harmless . . . without heavy religious overtones." See Kramer, *Christ,* 101 (#23*c*). Moreover, the only known milieu for *mar*-sayings is the eschatological expectation of the Aramaic-speaking community; Acts 2:36 certainly does not fit into this milieu.

[30] Thus Reginald Fuller, *The Foundations of New Testament Christology* (New York: Scribner's, 1965), 204-14, credits Phil. 2:9-11 to the "Hellenistic Gentile Mission." Fuller sees the bestowal of the title Lord as "the manifestation of a dignity heretofore hidden to and unacknowledged by the powers" (212). The opinion of Hahn, *Hoheitstitel,* 115-17, cited above, errs in setting up a false "either-or" dichot-

C. The statement of Acts 2:36 is probably the result of Luke's theological reflection.[31] It is evident that Luke was aware of credal statements which attributed Jesus' becoming Christ, Lord and son of God[32] to the resurrection. It is also evident that he was aware of credal statements which attributed these same titles to Jesus at his birth and even before.[33] His own conception attempts to harmonize these different credal statements: It is precisely because Jesus was son of God and messiah that he had to become Christ and Lord by the life and death foreordained by God and foretold in the scriptures.[34]

IV. *Functional christology.* Dupont has questioned the use of the labels "subordinationist" and "adoptionist" attached to theological viewpoints supposedly detected in Acts.[35] This anachronistic terminology only serves to confuse the issue; the speculative discussions which gave them birth were far removed from the concrete conceptions of the New Testament writers. He suggests that the term "functional christology" would better designate the viewpoint of Luke, a "subordinationist" viewpoint that seems to correspond to the thought of all New Testament authors.[36]

Conclusion. The christology of the discourse of Acts 2 faithfully reproduces the view held by the author himself of the role of Jesus in God's plan of salvation. The summarizing statement of Acts 2:36 is best explained, not as a pre-Lukan credal statement, but as the author's own attempt to synthesize the various credal statements he had received in the tradition.

---

omy. According to Hahn, Jesus is given the κύριος title in Acts 2:36 not because of his divine nature but because of his exaltation, which must somehow rule out the former.

[31] According to Kramer, *Christ*, 191-93 (#57d), only one text (Rom. 14:9) shows the possibility of a working together of the ideas underlying the titles by theological reflection on the part of Paul.

[32] Acts 13:33. See Eduard Schweizer, "The Concept of the Davidic 'Son of God' in Acts and Its Old Testament Background," *Studies in Luke-Acts*, 186-93.

[33] Statements in the infancy narrative (Luke 1:31-33, 35, 43; 2:11, 26ff.), which undoubtedly goes back to a pre-Lukan source, are clearly in this line of thought.

[34] O'Neill, *Theology*, 126f., offers the suggestion that Luke was attempting to reconcile two earlier ideas "to evolve a catholic theology."

[35] Dupont, "Discours," 55f. Cf. Schweizer, "Concept," 187.

[36] Wilckens, *Missionsreden*, 163, would seem to agree: "Der Titel [χριστός] bezeichnet bei Lukas die zentrale heilsgeschichtliche Funktion Jesu . . . also muss Gott es sein, der Jesus als sein zentrales heilsgeschichtliches Werkzug einsetzt und benutzt."

Early Traditions in Acts 3

The most cursory glance at the discourse of Acts 3 reveals the absence of key elements in the Lukan notion of how salvation is to be preached and achieved observable in the Acts as a whole. There is no mention of the Spirit, surprising in view of the proximity of the Pentecost-event, both in the supposed chronology and in the order of the book.[37] There is no community to be joined, and hence no baptism in the name of Jesus.

The hypothesis suggests itself that in the composition of the speech of Acts 3 Luke was following a source which, perhaps because it came from traditions that had survived from an earlier stage of the development of the community, did not contain these elements.[38] Several features of the discourse must now be considered, features which will give considerable support to the hypothesis.

The Role of Repentance

Peter calls his hearers to repentance in 3:19f.: μετανοήσατε οὖν καὶ ἐπιστρέψατε πρὸς τὸ ἐξαλειφθῆναι ὑμῶν τὰς ἁμαρτίας, ὅπως ἂν ἔλθωσιν καιροὶ ἀναψύξεως. . . . The people are called to repentance in order that the times of refreshment might come forth from the Lord; what they are awaiting depends on their repentance, on their turning from their sins.

I. *Jewish literature.* The argument of 3:19f. has many contacts in early Jewish literature:[39]

A. Rabbinical. Billerbeck lists a series of texts which illustrate this

---

[37] Lane, *Times of Refreshment,* 169-72, has suggested that καιροὶ ἀναψύξεως refers to the bestowal of the Spirit. But this suggestion depends on the questionable hypothesis that there is contact between the "Western" tradition of Acts 3:20 and a translation of Isa. 32:15 similar to that of Symmachus, and further that the "Western" tradition is to be preferred in Acts 3:20 (above, chap. 1, n. 118). Moreover, even if the suggestion is correct, it must be asked whether Luke understood such a reference to the Spirit; if he did, it is difficult to understand why he did not make it more evident to the reader. Thus, at least as far as the intention of Luke is concerned, there is no reference to the Spirit in the speech of Acts 3.

[38] Another hypothesis of course is quite possible, namely that Luke has not wished to repeat himself by including elements already mentioned in Acts 2. The analysis of the similarities of the two discourses undertaken in the last chapter already makes this highly unlikely. The following arguments make it even more unlikely.

[39] Cf. Lane, *Times of Refreshment,* 126-31.

notion of repentance in rabbinical literature.[40] The following are representative:

1. Sanh 97[b] records a discussion between R. Eliezer ben Hyrcanus (c. 90 C.E.) and R. Jehoshua ben Chanania over the time of the redemption or the liberation of Israel. The position of the former is given in the sentence: "If the Israelites repent, they will be redeemed; but if not, they will not be redeemed." [41]

2. R. Meir (middle of second century C.E.) compared God to a father who would forgive his son when the son had mended his evil ways: "If we repent, so will he have mercy on us and allow us to return to our country; but if we wander on evil paths, he will not allow us to return to our country" (Midr Abba Gorion, ed. Buber, Version 2, 41*a*).

3. R. Acha (c. 320 C.E.) said in the name of R. Tanchum ben Chiya (c. 300 C.E.): "If the Israelites would repent for one day, the son of David (messiah) would come immediately" (p Ta'an 1.1 [64[a]]).

B. "Intertestamental" Literature. The same idea is found in much earlier texts:

1. The Assumption of Moses, dated by Charles to the early part (7-30) of the first century C.E.,[42] implies the dependence of God's coming on the repentance of the people: ". . . that His name should be called upon until the day of repentance in the visitation[43] wherewith the Lord will visit them in the consummation of the end of days" (1:18). Moreover the significance of the strange figure, Taxo (chap. 9), lies, according to J. Licht,[44] in the fact that his penitential acts are intended to promote divine vengeance and deliverance. Thus "the end will come *because* vengeance shall finally be provoked" (97).

[40] *S-B* 1, 162*ff*.

[41] For an explanation of R. Eliezer's opinion, see further *S-B* 4, 992*c* and 1007. R. Jehoshua has the last word in the discussion, but Billerbeck notes that Rab (who died *c.* 247 C.E.) held the opinion of Eliezer.

[42] R. H. Charles, *The Assumption of Moses* (Oxford: Clarendon Press, 1897), 40-48 (introduction). This material is summarized in his edition of the *Pseudepigrapha* (Oxford: Clarendon Press, 1913), 411.

[43] Charles, *Assumption*, 8 (cf. *Pseudepigrapha*, 415), points out that *respicere-respectus* translate ἐπισκέπτειν which in turn translates *paqad*, which indicated a "visitation" that is often favorable in the Old Testament, and always favorable in the New.

[44] J. Licht, "Taxo, or the Apocalyptic Doctrine of Vengeance," *Journal of Jewish Studies* 12 (1961), 95-103.

2. Several passages in the Testaments of the Twelve Patriarchs[45] indicate the close connection between repentance and the in-breaking of the eschatological times; for example, Test. Dan. 6:4: "For he [the enemy] knows that on the day on which Israel shall repent [var., "believe"], the kingdom of the enemy shall be brought to an end." [46]

3. S. Mowinckel has argued that since Ps. Sol. 17 lays the responsibility for the disaster on the sins of the people and since the psalms constantly call for repentance, this may be the origin of the idea that the coming of the messiah "may be hastened by penitence and the fulfilling of the Law." [47]

C. The canonical scripture. In discussing the "utterances which make the coming of the Messiah conditional on repentance," G. F. Moore states: "This is the burden of the prophets from first to last; it is written in some of the most pertinent and impressive chapters of the Law." [48]

Thus the doctrine found in later Jewish writings is a natural evolution of the call to repentance by the prophets. As apocalyptic grew and the expectation of a divine intervention intensified, this final visitation of God became connected with the necessity for repentance—by repenting the people could hasten the day of the Lord.

II. *Early Christian literature.* According to Mark 1:15 the message of Jesus was not "Repent in order that the kingdom may come," but "Repent because the kingdom has come near." The notion that repentance will bring on the final divine intervention at the end of time (or at the coming of Jesus) is rarely found in the New Testament. Besides Acts 3:19f., the only text which reflects the notion is 2 Pet. 3:12 προσδοκῶντας καὶ σπεύδοντας τὴν παρουσίαν τῆς τοῦ θεοῦ ἡμέρας.[49]

[45] See the edition of R. H. Charles, *The Greek Versions of the Testaments of the Twelve Patriarchs* (Oxford: Clarendon Press, 1908).

[46] Cf. Test. Jud. 23:15, Test. Dan. 5:1-13.

[47] S. Mowinckel, *He That Cometh*, trans. G. W. Anderson (Oxford: Blackwell, 1956), 297.

[48] G. F. Moore, *Judaism* 2 (Cambridge: Harvard University Press, 1927), 350.

[49] H. Windisch, *Die katholischen Briefe*, 3rd ed., Handbuch zum Neuen Testament, vol. 15 (Tübingen: Mohr, 1951), 103f.: "σπεύδειν τὶ ist 'beschleunigen,' vgl. Herm Sim 9, 3, 2 (mit acc. c. inf.), abgeschwächt 'erstreben'. Vielleicht meint der Vf. den bekannten Gedanken, dass der Tag kommt, wenn die ganze Gemeinde Busse getan hat und geheiligt ist."

A. 2 Pet. 3:3*ff.* is an attempt by the author to answer the taunts of those who point to the long delay of the parousia. E. Käsemann[50] has demonstrated that the arguments of the author draw heavily upon Jewish apocalyptic ideas, and not upon the "Christian" ideas found in the rest of the New Testament. He sees in 2 Pet. 3:12 the Jewish notion of hastening the day of the coming of the Lord by repentance. D. von Allmen agrees that the Jewish origin of 2 Pet. 3:11*f.* cannot be doubted,[51] and points out that the concept taken over by the author in 3:11*f.* is not his own, which is proved by his replacement of σπεύδοντας by σπουδάσατε when he resumes the ideas in his own terms (263).

B. The conception of the author of 2 Peter. Von Allmen comes to the conclusion that the author of 2 Peter has robbed the time of Jesus of its eschatological character (273). The Jewish apocalyptic idea of the final day of Yahweh has been given a Christian interpretation in that the expected intervention would be the coming of Jesus. But the fundamental Jewish notion remains the same, that the great event is still to come. The people can prepare themselves for it and hasten its coming by repentance. Hence in 2 Pet. 3:4, 9, the promise (ἐπαγγελία) refers to something in the future, and the basic problem is the apparent delay in the fulfillment of the promise by the coming eschatological intervention of the Lord.

III. *The context of Acts 3:19f.* The conception of the author of 2 Peter is not that of Luke. To conceive the eschatology of Luke as realized eschatology is inaccurate, as Cadbury has pointed out.[52] A final intervention of God is still expected, though its imminence is no longer a factor. However it is equally inaccurate to say that the "last times" (cf. Acts 2:17) have in no way begun. The coming of Jesus represents a decisive event in God's plan. His salvific action in favor of his people can be expressed by the concept of promise (ἐπαγγελία) and fulfillment, and this

[50] E. Käsemann, "An Apologia for Primitive Christian Eschatology," *Essays on New Testament Themes,* trans. W. J. Montague, *SBT* 41 (1964), 169-95.

[51] D. von Allmen, "L'apocalyptique juive et le retard de la parousie en II Pierre 3, 1-13," *RTPhil* 99 (1966), 255-74.

[52] H. Cadbury, "Acts and Eschatology," *The Background of the New Testament and Its Eschatology* (Cambridge: University Press, 1956), 300-321. Cf. Conzelmann, *Theology,* 131*f.*

promise is now fulfilled with the glorification of Jesus Christ.[53]

If Luke does not propose the radical solution encountered in 2 Peter for the delay of the parousia, namely a deliberate return to Jewish apocalyptic ideas, the explanation of Acts 3:19f. must be sought in a different direction. It is to be noted that this Jewish appeal is quite at home in its surroundings. Peter addresses his auditors by singular flattering terms that stress their privileged role as members of the chosen people. He does not ask them to join some new community; he appeals to them as to the descendants of Abraham to whom the promised blessing has been sent in the preaching of repentance of Jesus Christ (3:26). As W. Furneaux has correctly observed: "Peter still thinks of the Kingdom as a national kingdom, the second advent depending on the conversion of the Jews. He has as yet no conception of the union of Jew and Gentile in one church. The return of the Lord would inaugurate the happy age for Israel, and he calls upon his hearers to hasten that return by accepting him." [54]

It would seem that Luke depends on sources in his construction of this appeal to the Jews. But it must not be too quickly concluded that these sources go back to the early Jerusalem community. The explanation lies at hand that Luke has used Jewish sources to compose what he thought would be a typical appeal of the early community to the Jews. While this highly complicated and improbable feat of archaizing must be judged the weaker hypothesis, it must not be deemed impossible for Luke.

Conclusion. Luke has adopted a Jewish appeal for repentance and placed it in congenial surroundings in a discourse directed to the Jews. The use of source material seems evident, but because of the possibility of successful archaizing the question of its primitive nature must remain open.

The Moses-Typology

The unusual titles for Jesus in the discourse of Acts 3 were seen to

---

[53] In Luke 24:49 and Acts 1:4 the promise is evidently still to come; in Acts 2:33, 39 it has come in the sending of the Spirit. In 13:32, the promise is fulfilled in the sending of Jesus as Savior; in 26:6 the promise is fulfilled in the resurrection of Jesus, a pledge of the resurrection of the faithful. Hence in Acts the promise is fulfilled in the Jesus-event.

[54] W. Furneaux, *The Acts of the Apostles* (Oxford: Clarendon Press, 1912), 56.

have been derived most likely from a Moses-Jesus typology. The typology, however, extends far beyond the mere use of titles:

I. *The Moses-Jesus parallel of Acts 3 and 7.* The discourses of Acts 3 and 7 complete each other in presenting an extended parallel between Moses and Jesus:

A. Links between chapters 3 and 7.

1. Deut. 18:15, the text on which the hope for a prophet like Moses was based,[55] is found only in these two discourses (3:22; 7:37) in "orthodox" Christian literature before the end of the second century.[56]

2. Exod. 3:6 is quoted in 7:32 and alluded to in 3:13 in a form slightly different from its only other use in the New Testament, namely in the question concerning the resurrection in Mark 12:26 pars. (pp. 44-47).

3. The verb ἀρνεῖσθαι of denying one sent by God occurs in Luke-Acts only in these two discourses, in 3:14 for Jesus and in 7:35 for Moses.

4. Similar titles are used for Jesus (3:14 δίκαιος; 3:15 ἀρχηγός) and Moses (7:27, 35 ἄρχων καὶ δικαστής).

5. The return of Jesus, for which there is a parallel in the presentation of the life of Moses in Acts 7, is mentioned only in 3:20*f.* in Acts.

6. The Moses-Jesus parallel is absent from the other discourses, indeed from the rest of Acts.[57]

[55] According to H. Teeple, *The Mosaic Eschatological Prophet,* JBL Monograph Series 10 (1957), 43-48, the notion of Moses as eschatological prophet was not connected with Deut. 18:15 at first. It rather came from two other sources: (1) expectation of the return of Mosaic times; (2) extension of the belief that Elijah having ascended to heaven would come again. In any event, the hope was soon closely connected to the Deuteronomy passage.

[56] Irenaeus cites Acts 3 according to the "Western" tradition in *Against Heresies* 3.12.3. But Clement of Alexandria may depend directly on Deut. 18:15, 19 in *The Instructor* 1:7, since a reference to Lev. 23:29 is missing. Tertullian, *Against Marcion* 4.22.10, has a text similar to Acts 3:22 in that Deut. 18:15 is linked with Lev. 23:29, but the text differs significantly from such "Western" witnesses as Irenaeus and h. Otherwise there are no references to Deut. 18:15 among second century "orthodox" writers. Citations of Deut. 18:15 in the Pseudo-Clementine literature will be considered below.

[57] According to Wilcox, *Semitisms,* 162f., there is a subtle reference in the wording of the logion of John Baptist in Paul's Pisidian Antioch speech (13:25), which is influenced by the citation of Exod. 3:5 in Acts 7:33. While this citation differs slightly from the Septuagint and may indicate a special Greek source used in both places in Acts, it hardly points to a Moses-Jesus parallel in Paul's speech. As J. Manek, "The New Exodus in the Books of Luke," *NovT* 2 (1957/1958), 8-23,

7. In both speeches, the Jews are referred to the covenant of God with Abraham (3:25; 7:2-8, 17).[58]

   These contacts are hardly coincidental, and indicate a common conception lying behind the Moses-references in the two speeches. To determine the extent and meaning of the typology it will be necessary to consider the material of both discourses.

B. The extended parallel of Acts 7.[59] The most striking single feature of the Moses-Jesus parallel of Acts 7 is the reference to Moses as δυνατός ἐν λόγοις καὶ ἔργοις αὐτοῦ (7:22).[60] Elsewhere in Luke-Acts this expression is used only of Jesus, when the disciples on the way to Emmaus declare that he was an ἀνὴρ προφήτης δυνατὸς ἐν ἔργῳ καὶ λόγῳ (Luke 24:19). But it is the manner in which the life of Moses is presented that makes the intention of the speaker (author) plain—their rejection of Jesus is similar to their fathers' rejection of Moses (7:51):

1. The youthful Moses is said to have been instructed (ἐπαιδεύθη) in the wisdom of Egypt (7:22); the child (παιδίον) Jesus is twice declared to have grown in wisdom in Luke's infancy narrative (Luke 2:40, 52).

2. Moses attempts to bring salvation to his people, but they do not understand that he is from God (7:25), and he is forced to flee from them (7:29). Later (7:35) the people are said to have denied (ἠρνήσαντο) Moses. Similarly Jesus is sent by God to the Jews (3:26) but through ignorance (3:17) they deny him (3:14 ὑμεῖς δὲ τὸν ἅγιον καὶ δίκαιον ἠρνήσασθε).

3. Moses is favored by a theophany on Mount Sinai; then he is sent as leader and liberator of the people (7:35). He predicts that God will raise up a prophet like himself in the future (7:37).[61] But the people again reject his "living words" (7:

---

has shown, this speech of Paul contains the only clear example of a Moses-Jesus antithesis in Luke-Acts, namely the reference to the powerlessness of the Law of Moses in 13:38f. See the discussion below, p. 83.

[58] J. Bihler, *Die Stephanusgeschichte*, 104, concludes: "Diese Rede [Acts 3] enthält eine ganze Reihe von Parallelen zur Stephanusrede, und sie dürfte deshalb für das Verständnis der Heilsvorstellungen in der Stephanusrede einiges beitragen."

[59] Cf. J. Jeremias, "Μωϋσῆς," *TDNT* 4, 868 n. 226.

[60] The phrase may be inspired by Exod. 4:15-17 in which Yahweh promises to be with Moses through his words and his works (σημεῖα).

[61] This element corresponds to the return of Jesus which is foretold in Acts 3:20f.

39-43). Moses' ascent on Mount Sinai would seem to correspond to Jesus' ascending to the Father after his death.[62] He is sent again to the people as leader and savior through the preaching of the apostles (3:13-15, 22-26, cf. 5:31), and his return is foretold (Acts 3:20*f.*). But the Jews are in the process of rejecting him again, as is demonstrated by the execution of Stephen and the persecution of the community in Jerusalem.

Thus, the story of the life of Moses of Acts 7 is a close parallel to the Jesus-kerygma of Acts 3. The point of the comparison is clear: the danger that the people will reject Jesus a second time as they rejected Moses.

C. Special features of chapter 3. While the greater part of the actual "Moses" material is contained in Acts 7, there are features of Acts 3 which point to the Moses typology in their own right. The unusual titles have already been treated. In addition, the reference to Jesus as the προκεχειρισμένον[63] messiah (3:20) may have overtones of Moses typology.[64] The response of Moses to Yahweh's command to go to Pharaoh on behalf of the people is: προχείρισαι δυνάμενον ἄλλον, ὅν ἀποστελεῖς (Exod. 4:13). Connecting this to Deut. 18:15 cited in Acts 3:22, it is evident how Jesus can be referred to in Moses typology as the προκεχειρισμένον χριστόν.

II. *The primitive nature of the material.* The extended Moses-Jesus parallel interwoven so essentially into the fabric of Acts 3 and 7, yet totally absent from the rest of Acts, is probably to be credited to source material of a primitive nature.

A. The meaning of the parallel. The parallel drawn between the mission of Moses and that of Jesus consists principally in the fact that both were rejected by the people, but then reconfirmed in their office as savior of the people by God, only to be rejected again. The key text which serves as the basis of the parallel, Deut. 18:15, qualifies Jesus as the prophet like Moses

---

[62] Georg Kretschmar, "Himmelfahrt und Pfingsten," *Zeitschrift für Kirchengeschichte* 66 (1954/1955), 217-22, presents evidence from iconography that Moses' ascent of Sinai to receive the Law and Jesus' ascension were depicted in a strikingly similar manner in the earliest known Christian representations. See the further discussion in chap. 3, n. 62.

[63] In the New Testament only Acts 3:20; 22:14; 26:16.

[64] Descamps, *Les justes*, 72.

foretold by the latter before his death. In each case we have the figure of the persecuted or rejected prophet.

Descamps has distinguished clearly the notions of "persecuted prophet" and "suffering just one." [65] The latter has a note of passivity: The innocent sufferer submits to his fate and renders his sufferings efficacious by accepting them. But the prophet has power from God to accomplish a mission among the people. For him contradictions and persecutions are obstacles to be overcome; it is not because of them, but in spite of them that he accomplishes his mission. Thus Jesus is the prophet like Moses; and like Moses he is rejected by the people. [66]

B. Contacts in late Judaism. In late Judaism there was a lively expectation of a prophet. [67] The hope took various forms, some of which show affinity to the Moses-Jesus typology of Acts 3 and 7:

1. Prophet as Forerunner. The classic figure of the prophet as forerunner of the day of the Lord was Elijah, whose popularity in the ancient synagogue was immense. [68] Elijah-speculation was based in large part on Mal. 3:23, in which God declares he will send Elijah to prepare his people before the coming of the great day of the Lord. In the "intertestamental" literature, however, the place of Elijah is decidedly secondary. [69] Except for a cryptic reference in 1 Enoch 89:51f. and an allusion in 4 Ezra 6:25f., he is not mentioned at all. The principal witness for the importance of Elijah-speculation at the time is the New Testament itself. Mark 9:11-13 reports that in the opinion of the scribes the coming of Elijah must precede the kingdom. [70] And in Mark 6:14f., some people think that Jesus is Elijah, an opinion expressed also for John Baptist according to John 1:21. The possible influence of Elijah-speculation on Acts 3:19-21 will be considered later in this chapter.

---

[65] *Ibid.,* 77.

[66] Cf. Mowinckel, *He That Cometh,* 329.

[67] O. Michel, "Spätjüdisches Prophetentum," *Neutestamentliche Studien für R. Bultmann,* 60-66.

[68] *S-B* 4 (2) , 764.

[69] *Ibid.,* 780.

[70] R. Bultmann, *History of the Synoptic Tradition,* trans. J. Marsh (Oxford: Blackwell, 1963) , 260, points out that Mark 9:11 should follow 9:1, Jesus' saying about the coming of the kingdom. The evangelist has inserted the transfiguration story.

2. Interpreter of the Law. In 1 Macc. 4:46; 14:41 a prophet is awaited to solve certain difficult religious questions.[71] The community at Qumran regarded the interpretation of the torah as its chief task;[72] the sect's teacher had special understanding of the torah valid for the last times.[73] Rabbinic traditions speak of an interpretation of the torah in the messianic times.[74] The hope for an eschatological interpretation of the torah, which has almost certainly influenced Matthew,[75] seems not to have left its trace on the Moses typology of Acts 3 and 7.

3. Popular Hope. Josephus claims that the Essenes had the power to prophesy about future events; they seldom missed in their predictions.[76] He reports the evil done by false prophets during the siege of Jerusalem.[77] Moreover, the popular leaders of uprisings before the final revolt styled themselves as prophets: Theudas[78] and the Egyptian Jew[79] may be mentioned.

While the hope for a prophet-leader was undoubtedly strong among the people, it is not certain that this leader was identified with Moses.[80] Two facts, however, point in this direction. First, the role assigned to Moses in Palestinian Judaism was chiefly that of intermediary of God's revelation.[81] The Assumption of Moses (11:16) calls him *divinum per orbem terrarum profeten,* which Charles interprets as meaning "the prophet for the whole world," claiming that a Hebrew superlative lies behind this Latin translation.[82] Secondly, the axiom was later to be accepted among the rabbis: "As the first

---

[71] Teeple, *Prophet,* 3-9, argues convincingly that Elijah is not specifically intended here.

[72] IQS 6:6*f.;* 8:11*ff.;* CD 6:9; the numerous fragments of *pesharim* testify to the reality of these prescriptions.

[73] IQpHab 7.

[74] *S-B* 4 (1) , 1*ff.* Cf. Teeple, *Prophet,* 21*f.*

[75] W. D. Davies, *The Setting of the Sermon on the Mount* (Cambridge: The University Press, 1966) , 188*f.*

[76] *War* 2. (8.12) .159.

[77] *War* 6. (5.2) .286*f.*

[78] *Antiq.* 20. (5.1) . 97*f.;* cf. Acts 5:36*f.*

[79] *Antiq.* 20. (8.6) . 169-72; cf. Acts 21:38.

[80] R. Schnackenburg, "Die Erwartung des 'Propheten' nach dem Neuen Testament und den Qumran-Texten," *Studia Evangelica,* TU 73 (1959) , 622-39, agrees that there was some kind of prophetic expectation among the people, but ill-defined.

[81] Jeremias, "Μωϋσῆς," 848-74.

[82] Charles, *Assumption,* 47.

savior (Moses), so the last (messiah) "; a corollary was the belief that the messiah would come from the desert as Moses had.[83] Jeremias sees such a belief already in first century Judaism in the Egyptian who is said to have begun a revolt after coming out of the desert (Acts 21:38), and in the warning of Matt. 24:26, that if messianic pretenders should arise in the desert (ἰδοὺ ἐν τῇ ἐρήμῳ ἐστίν) the disciples should not go out to them.[84]

4. Qumran. 4QTest,[85] is a leaf containing four scriptural citations, which pronounce eschatological destruction to be visited upon four classes of people: Those who do not listen to the prophet; the enemies of the star and the scepter; the opponents of the Levitical priesthood; and the inhabitants of a city which had been rebuilt under a curse. The first passage dealing with the prophet is a quotation of Deut. 5:28 and 18:18f. Deut. 18:19 is cited in Acts 3:23.

5. Samaritan Belief. Because of their peculiar notion of prophet as spokesman of God, who knows at first hand the divine will, the Samaritans recognized no prophets other than Moses. However they did await the coming of a figure, called *Taheb* (the "restorer"), who would bring victory to the elect in the world. Eventually Taheb became regarded as a *Moses redivivus*.[86]

The possibility of Samaritan influence on Acts 7 is strongly urged by M. Scharlemann.[87] He presents fifteen contacts between the speech of Stephen and Samaritan beliefs and textural traditions whose cumulative effect is certainly convincing. The same author concludes his study by declaring that Stephen was "something of an isolated theological figure in the story of the primitive church" who "addressed himself to a particular problem, the issue of Samaria." Hence it may be concluded that Luke has respected the primitive nature of

---

[83] *S-B* 1, 85-88.

[84] Jeremias, "Μωϋσῆς," 859-62.

[85] J. M. Allegro, "Further Messianic References in Qumran Literature," *JBL* 75 (1956), 174-87.

[86] John Macdonald, *The Theology of the Samaritans*, The New Testament Library (Philadelphia: Westminster Press, 1964), 205, 362.

[87] Martin H. Scharlemann, *Stephen: A Singular Saint* (Rome: Pontifical Biblical Institute, 1968), 36-51.

the tradition he received, and that the discourse is "an authentic echo of the theological position of Stephen." [88]

C. Moses in early Christianity. A survey of the New Testament material leads Teeple[89] to conclude that two types of traditions must be distinguished, those in which Jesus is conceived as the prophet *like* Moses, and those in which he is *unlike* Moses because he is held to be far superior to him. The latter motif developed as the breach between Christianity and Judaism widened, and may be found in Paul, Hebrews,[90] and the fourth gospel.[91]

Other early Christian works, however, present a wide variety of approaches to the relative roles of Moses and Jesus:

1. Mark. Moses-typology occurs in the gospel of Mark only in the story of the transfiguration.[92] How much the typology is due to Mark and how much is due to pre-Markan traditions must remain conjectural, but the mention of Elijah before Moses in 9:4, unique in the accounts of the transfiguration, tells against a Markan interest in Moses typology. Further, there is an example of the later antithetical relation between

---

[88] *Ibid.,* 185*f.* A discussion of the many opinions relative to Stephen and his speech is beyond the scope of this work. Many opposing theories have been offered to explain the "hellenists." Thus Oscar Cullmann, "The Significance of the Qumran Texts for Research into the Beginnings of Christianity," *JBL* 74 (1955), 213-26 (reprinted in K. Stendahl, *The Scrolls and the NT* (New York: Harper, 1957), 18-32), was of the opinion that there was a connection between an early hellenistic group in the community and the Qumran sect. Matthew Black, *The Scrolls and Christian Origins* (New York: Scribner's, 1961), 75-77, refuted Cullmann's thesis, and suggested that the line between Qumran and the community should be traced through the "Hebrews." Georgi, *Gegner,* 217, finds traces of the θεῖος ἀνήρ representation of hellenistic Judaism. A persistent theme in criticism is the association of Stephen's speech with "Alexandrian" thought. B. W. Bacon, "Stephen's Speech: Its Argument and Doctrinal Relationship," *Biblical and Semitic Studies* (New York: Scribner's, 1901), 213-76, one of the most noted proponents of the theory, admitted that "Alexandrianism" need in no way imply a non-Palestinian origin. But Scharlemann has convincingly demonstrated the flimsy bases of the supposed Alexandrian contacts of the speech. Marcel Simon, *St. Stephen and the Hellenists in the Primitive Church* (London: Longmans, 1958), who regards Stephen as a proponent of a type of reformed Judaism, notes the similarities to Samaritan thought. He denies that Stephen belongs to the same thought world as Hebrews or Barnabas, but sees the true legacy of his thought among the Ebionites. See below pp. 86-88.

[89] Teeple, *Prophet,* 94-97; Simon, *St. Stephen,* 60*f.*

[90] Jeremias, "Μωϋσῆς," 871.

[91] Teeple, *Prophet,* 96, argues that John 5:46 and 3:13-15 are not examples of prophet-like-Moses typology for Jesus.

[92] Cf. Jeremias, "Μωϋσῆς," 869 n. 228.

Moses and Jesus in the matter of divorce (10:3), and pointedly in the discussion concerning the resurrection (12:19).

2. Matthew. W. D. Davies argues that the Moses typology of the gospel of Matthew must be understood in the light of the Jewish expectation of a Moses-like figure who would interpret the torah in the end time. Jesus is not the giver of a new law; but as the giver of the eschatological interpretation of the law he is the "ultimate figure," the "new and greater Moses." [93]

Two remarks are in order: First, the understanding of Matthew derives from Jewish thought. Second, by emphasizing the role of Jesus as the "new and greater Moses" it is already on the way between a view of Jesus as the prophet *like* Moses and the view of Jesus as an eschatological figure *unlike* Moses, because superior to him.

The reason for the shift in the understanding of the Moses-Jesus relationship lies in the growing self-understanding of the new community as a new dispensation over against Judaism in God's plan. Since "mediator" was "a recognized title of his (Moses) in the first century of the Christian era," [94] it was but a step to the conclusion that a superior covenant would need a superior mediator.

3. Luke. Attempts to find a special Moses typology in the gospel of Luke have not met with success. J. Manek claimed evidence for an exodus typology in the third gospel and the beginning of Acts, [95] but the evidence is slim and unconvincing, as M. Sabbe has pointed out. [96] C. F. Evans offered the hypothesis that the ordering of materials in the "central section" of the gospel follows the ordering of materials in Deut. 1–26; [97] F. Gils has demonstrated the tenuous nature of the hypothesis. [98]

[93] Davies, *The Sermon on the Mount* (Cambridge: The University Press, 1966), 35.

[94] Charles, *Assumption*, 6, commenting on 1.14. The title is also attested in Philo (*Life of Moses* 3.18) and frequently in the Talmud.

[95] Manek, "New Exodus," 13*ff*.

[96] M. Sabbe, "La rédaction du récit de la transfiguration," *La Venue du Messie*, Rech Bib 6 (1962), 65-100, specifically rejects the hypothesis of Manek (93 n. 2).

[97] C. F. Evans, "The Central Section of St. Luke's Gospel," *Studies in the Gospels: Essays in Memory of R. H. Lightfoot*, ed. D. E. Nineham (Oxford: Blackwell, 1955), 37-53.

[98] F. Gils, *Jésus Prophète d'après les évangiles synoptiques*, Orientalia et Biblica Lovaniensia 2 (Louvain: Publications Universitaires, 1957), 41*f*.

4. 1 Clement. Moses-Jesus typology is patently not within the thought structure of the author of the letter of the Church of Rome to the Church of Corinth, for Moses is not to be placed on the same plane as Jesus. He is said to have suffered through jealousy as other heroes of ancient and modern times (4.10, 12); his foresight in adjudicating claims to authority is compared to the same foresight on the part of the apostles (43-44); and his prayer for the people before God is held up as a model for those who love peace (53-54). Thus Moses is a type and model for those who have exercised and do exercise authority in the church, but no Moses-Jesus parallel is drawn or even hinted at.

5. Barnabas. In the Epistle of Barnabas there are traditions which might at first glance appear to constitute a Moses-Jesus typology. In 12:1-7 an image of the cross is found in Moses' holding his arms up to give Israel victory over Amalek, and in his constructing the bronze serpent. However, these figures do not see a parallel between the *mission* of Moses and that of Jesus, but rather in incidental events whose relation to Jesus are peripheral at best.[99] Actually Moses stands in contrast to Jesus with regard to his central mission, for although he truly spoke God's word the people did not understand (10:1*f.*, 9, 11), and rejected the covenant offered to them through his meditation (4.6-8=14.1*ff.*). The superiority of Christianity lies in the fact that Christians have truly received the covenant through Jesus.

6. Justin. The two instances of the prefiguration of the cross in the life of Moses found in the Epistle of Barnabas occur also in Justin's *Dialogue* (chaps. 90-91). Justin regards Moses as a true prophet (*Apology* 32) and law-giver. Not all of the Mosaic law is still valid for Christians, for some of the regulations were given only on account of the hardness of heart of the Jews (*Dialogue* 27, 45), which in no way diminishes the greatness of Moses. However there is no Moses typology in Justin in the sense of Acts 3 and 7.

7. Κηρύγματα Πέτρου. It is generally agreed among scholars

[99] Kraft, *Barnabas*, 118*f.*, argues that Barnabas goes deeper than merely mechanical typology in citing these images, being more interested in the suffering and saving represented by the cross. It is, however, evidently not the central thrust of the mission of Moses which is paralleled to that of Jesus.

that the fourth century Pseudo-Clementine Recognitions and Homilies go back to a basic writing which probably originated in Syria in the third century.[100] Opinions concerning the basic writing, its use, and its sources, are divided. Since at least two distinct and widely differing views of the Jesus-Moses relationship seem to be present in the literature, source analysis must play an essential role in any attempt to explain them. In the following discussion the conclusions of G. Strecker's *Das Judenchristentum in den Pseudoklementinen* will be followed.[101]

As one of the sources of the basic writing, Strecker outlines the Κηρύγματα Πέτρου which he calls the ΚΠ-source.[102] Peculiar to this writing is the notion of the "true prophet," who first appeared in Adam, then reappeared in the great figures of Jewish history, to reach final fulfillment in Jesus, who gives the correct interpretation of the law.[103] Naturally, one of the representatives of true prophecy was Moses, and in one place the ΚΠ-source seems to have paralleled the missions of Jesus and Moses.[104] However, there is no Moses-Jesus typology in the manner of Acts 3 and 7.[105] Although Deut. 18:15, 19 is cited,[106] it is used to contrast Jesus with the prophets of old: he brings the truth to which they never attained (IIom. 3.53). The prophets on the whole are not highly regarded in the ΚΠ-source—there is only one reference to the canonical prophets (Hom. 16.7, a composite citation of Isaiah), and when Matt. 5:17 is quoted, Jesus says that he has come not to destroy the law, the reference to not destroying the prophets being omitted (Hom. 3.51).

[100] Hans Joachim Schoeps, *Jewish Christianity*, trans. Douglas R. A. Hare (Philadelphia: Fortress Press, 1964), 17; J. Irmscher, "The Pseudo-Clementines," trans. George Ogg, Hennecke-Schneemelcher, 2, 532-35.

[101] Georg Strecker, *Das Judenchristentum in den Pseudoklementinen*, TU 70 (1958).

[102] The existence of the ΚΠ-source is generally admitted. See Irmscher, "The Pseudo-Clementines," 533; Schoeps, *Jewish Christianity*, 16.

[103] See the summary by Georg Strecker, "The Kerygmata Petrou," Hennecke-Schneemelcher, 2, 107.

[104] According to Hom. 8.5-7, Moses is the teacher of God's truth to the Jews, as Jesus is to the Gentiles. Jews or Gentiles of good faith may be saved through Moses or Jesus respectively, but it is better to know and follow both.

[105] Strecker, *Judenchristentum*, 150.

[106] The form of the quotation differs from that of Acts 3:22f., in that the Deuteronomy passage is not combined with Lev. 23:29.

According to H. J. Schoeps, the doctrine of the ΚΠ-source is the result of an association by the Ebionites of the new Moses theme "with an Adam-myth derived from the heterodox Judaism of that time." [107] Whatever the cause, the "true prophet" doctrine of the ΚΠ-source—which is probably to be dated to the beginning of the third century[108]—has little in common with the Moses-Jesus typology of Acts 3 and 7.

8. Ἀναβαθμοὶ Ἰακώβου. Strecker has isolated a passage in the Clementine Recognitions (1.33-44; 1.53-71, except for 1.63 and minor interpolations), whose basic concepts differ widely from those of the rest of the Pseudo-Clementines.[109] In this passage the value of circumcision is not questioned, and in place of the radical opposition of the ΚΠ-source to sacrifices[110] there is a condemnation of the temple, whose construction is traced to the ambition of the kings.[111]

This attitude is strikingly similar to the attitude taken in Stephen's speech (Acts 7:44-50).[112] Moreover, parallels between this passage in the Recognitions and the Moses-Jesus typology of Acts 3 and 7 are not wanting. Moses is said to have foretold the coming of the *Christus aeternus* (Rec. 1.43). Deut. 18:15, 19 is combined with Lev. 23:29 in speaking of the prophet-like Moses as in Acts 3:22f. (Rec. 1.36). James is made to prove the "two advents" of the Christ from the scriptures (Rec. 1.68). Most important of all there is a paralleling of the miracles worked by Moses with those of Jesus (Rec. 1. 36, 56-58), one passage speaking of the *signa et prodigia* (cf. Acts 7:36 τέρατα καὶ σημεῖα) worked by Moses and Jesus (Rec. 1.57). It is true that in one passage Bartholomew is made to declare that Jesus as Christ is superior to Moses (Rec. 1.59), but this statement does not set the tone for the whole pas-

---

[107] Schoeps, *Jewish Christianity*, 68.

[108] Strecker, *Judenchristentum*, 218-20.

[109] *Ibid.*, 223-50.

[110] According to the ΚΠ-source, God has no need of sacrifices. References to sacrifices in the Law are "false pericopes," due to the female prophetic principle, enemy of the true prophet. See Strecker, "The Kerygmata Petrou," 107f.

[111] Rec. 1.38. *Ubi vero tyrannos sibi magis quaesivere quam reges, tunc etiam in loco, qui eis orationis causa fuerat praedestinatus, templum pro ambitione regia construxere, et sic per ordinem regibus impiis sibi invicem succedentibus, ad majores impietates etiam populus declinavit.*

[112] M. Simon, "La prophétie de Nathan et le temple (Remarques sur 2 Sam. 7)," *RHPhilRel* 32 (1952), 41-58.

sage, in which the similarity of Moses and Jesus is the central theme.

Strecker sees a close parallel to this passage of the Recognitions in a brief statement by Epiphanius describing the Ἀναβαθμοὶ ᾽Ιακώβου, a book containing stories about James of Jerusalem in the possession of the Ebionites (*Against Heresies* 30.16). The work alluded to by Epiphanius agrees with the Recognitions passage in opposing the temple, in describing "ascents" to the temple, and in opposing the apostle Paul. Hence Strecker calls the Recognitions passage the AJ II-source, dating it to approximately 150 c.e., and noting its possible connection to Pella.[113]

Whether or not Strecker's analysis be correct in every detail, the "AJ II-source" does seem to give evidence of a stream of "Jewish Christianity" [114] whose thought world may be described as a further development from that of the source of Acts 3 and 7.

Schoeps, also referring to Epiphanius, has called this section of the Recognitions part of an Ebionite Acts of the Apostles.[115] He finds in Rec. 1.35-38 the closest parallel in the early Christian literature to the speech of Stephen in Acts 7.[116] Although the parallels are not close enough to be entirely convincing, his argument may be taken as independent witness to the similarity between the thought worlds of an early stream of "Jewish Christianity" and the source of Acts 3 and 7.[117]

Thus the Moses-Jesus parallel of Acts 3 and 7, absent from later developments in the "orthodox" church, would seem to find its place in Palestinian traditions which were later taken up and developed in Jewish-Christian circles. To Luke these traditions probably seemed "primitive," worthy of being

[113] Strecker, *Judenchristentum*, 253f.

[114] Georg Strecker, "Zum Problem des Judenchristentums," appendix to W. Bauer's *Rechtgläubigkeit und Ketzerei im ältesten Christentum*, 2nd ed., Beiträge zur historischen Theologie 10 (Tübingen: Mohr, 1964), 245-48, points out that it is incorrect to speak simplistically of "Jewish Christianity" as some kind of unified and identifiable movement or group in early Christianity.

[115] Schoeps, *Jewish Christianity*, 16f.

[116] Hans Joachim Schoeps, *Theologie und Geschichte des Judenchristentums* (Tübingen: Mohr, 1949), 440-45.

[117] It is noteworthy that Rec. 1.54 mentions the Samaritan expectation of a prophet based on the predictions of Moses.

located in a speech given by Peter in the earliest days of the community.

Conclusion. The presentation of Jesus as the prophet like Moses in Acts 3 and 7 is unique in the early literature of "orthodox" Christianity. The most reasonable explanation is that this earlier typology, prepared by the Mosaic messiah and eschatological prophet expectations of the period, was forced into the background when the break with Judaism caused mainstream Christian writers to stress the superiority of Jesus over Moses. This explanation is supported by the probable influence of early Samaritan traditions on the speech of Stephen.

III. *Luke's use of this Moses typology.* F. Gils has convincingly pointed out the importance of the theme of Jesus-prophet in Luke; he distinguishes eight prophetic themes in Luke, most of which are proper to the third gospel.[118] Moreover Luke insists on the rejection of Jesus by the Jews. He opens the first stage of the ministry of Jesus with his rejection in his hometown (4:16-30). Similarly the second stage begins with a rejection in a town of the Samaritans (9:51-56). Finally, the passion account in Luke brings the rejection to its inevitable conclusion; literary contacts connect the death of Jesus to his first rejection in Nazareth.[119]

Outside of Acts 3 and 7, Moses typology hardly appears; the leading role in the prophetic themes is played by Elijah typology. But the Moses-Jesus parallel fitted well with Luke's own view-

[118] Gils, *Prophète*, 41f.

[119] Literary contacts: (1) Luke 23:1: καὶ ἀναστὰν ἅπαν τὸ πλῆθος αὐτῶν ἤγαγον αὐτὸν (resumed in 23:26: καὶ ὡς ἀπήγαγον αὐτὸν). Cf. 4:29: καὶ ἀναστάντες (4:28 πάντες) ἐξέβαλον αὐτόν . . . καὶ ἤγαγον αὐτόν. (2) In 23:37 Jesus is challenged by the mockers to save himself (σῶσον σεαυτόν), which recalls the logion cited by Jesus in 4:23 about the prophet in his πατρίς: θεράπευσον σεαυτόν. But the use of λαός in the Lukan passion account underlines the connection between the rejection of Jesus in his πατρίς and the ultimate rejection on Calvary:

Patris (Luke 4:16-30)	*Calvary* (Luke 23)
His townspeople	His people (the Chosen People)
scandalized at his claim	scandalized at his claim
to fulfill the prophecy of Isaiah	to be the Christ
scorn him (cure yourself)	scorn him (save yourself)
and lead him forth from their town	and lead him forth from their capital
to the hill on which it is built	to the place called the skull, evidently some kind of hill,
to kill him.	to kill him.

point that Jesus was a prophet rejected by the Jews. Hence he was able to work this early tradition harmoniously into his over-all scheme.

The same manner of employing early traditions is probably to be seen in Luke's use of the unusual repentance theme of 3:19*f.* studied above. The call to repentance is a feature of the apostolic preaching as presented by Luke. Though he recognized the appeal to the Jews of 3:19*f.* as incomplete in comparison with his own developed notion, he saw it as congenial to the picture of Christian beginnings in Jerusalem that he wished to paint.

The Christology of Acts 3

The presence of early tradition in the discourse of Acts 3 points in the direction of J. A. T. Robinson's claim that it contains the earliest christology to be found in the New Testament. Detailed analysis of the speech confirms this evaluation of the material:

I. *The Jesus-event in Acts 3*. Rearranging in logical order the state-ments of Acts 3 about Jesus gives the following outline of the Jesus-event:

A. Jesus as the servant was first sent by God to turn his people from their sins (3:25*f.*). He is the prophet foretold by Moses, the prophet who was to prepare the chosen people for the eschatological intervention of God (3:22).

B. Through his suffering he was perfected as the messiah (3:18).[120] The people brought about this suffering by their rejection of him (3:13*b*-15); but they acted through ignorance and can still repent (3:17, 19).

C. God has glorified his servant (3:13*a*); thus Jesus is now in heaven awaiting the messianic times for which his preaching was to prepare the people (3:21).

[120] According to J. A. T. Robinson, "Christology," 181-83, Jesus is only the Christ-elect in Acts 3, except for 3:18 which says that he suffered *as the Christ:* "Consciously or unconsciously, Luke is bringing this primitive summary with its heterodox theology into line with his own Christology." Moule, "Christology," makes the common-sense observation that Robinson's opinion "suggests an unlikely coupling of a reverence for ancient tradition with an arbitrary reversal of its meaning" (168). The solution would seem to be that for Luke, being the messiah necessarily involves a process with different stages (pp. 68-70). Luke is probably harmonizing different christological statements he has received (n. 34), but he does not contradict them.

D. The significance of Jesus now is that the people must hear his call to repentance; whoever does not listen to his words will be cut off from the people and will not participate in the days of refreshment (3:23). All the prophets have foretold these days of ultimate decision before the eschatological intervention by God (3:24).

E. In the future God will send Jesus again in the messianic times as the messiah (3:20). But the precise role of Jesus as the messiah is not delineated.

F. Acts 3:16 is omitted in this outline. Luke has formulated it to link the discourse to the event which preceded it, but it has little bearing on the role of Jesus as presented in the discourse:

1. While certain elements of the healing story (3:1-12a) may reflect elements of early tradition,[121] the vocabulary and style of Luke are evident in every verse. The similarity of this miracle of Peter to a cure by Paul in Acts 14:8-10 indicates the stylized nature of the narration.[122]

2. That Luke has fashioned 3:16 to connect discourse with event is clear from his repetition of the rare verb στερεοῦν (cf. 3:7) and his mention of the ὄνομα-theme (3:6). However, non-Lukan elements such as ἡ πίστις ἡ δι' αὐτοῦ [123] and ἀπέναντι [124] and the ungainly construction of the verse may indicate that he was not entirely free of sources in this passage.

3. In any event the ὄνομα-theme belongs to the narrative, not to the discourse. As has been pointed out above, neither the

[121] The first part of Peter's reply (3:6: Ἀργύριον καὶ χρυσίον οὐχ ὑπάρχει μοι) sounds like the remembrance of a short logion. The fact that it is in the singular indicates its originality, as the figure of John seems to be definitely a secondary addition to the narrative. See O. Bauernfeind, *Die Apostelgeschichte*, Theologischer Handkommentar zum Neuen Testament 5 (Leipzig: Deichert, 1939), 59. Also the location may reflect an early tradition: The Beautiful Gate is mentioned nowhere else in the New Testament (but two different words are used for it in 3:2, 10, which argues against a written source); The Porch of Solomon is mentioned eleswhere only in John 10:23, where the spelling is different, and Acts 5:12, which may well be secondary.

[122] Cf. C. S. C. Williams, *The Acts of the Apostles*, Black's New Testament Commentaries (London: Black, 1957), 170; J. Fenton, "The Order of the Miracles performed by Peter and Paul in Acts," *ExpT* 77 (1965/1966), 382.

[123] Elsewhere in Acts πίστις is followed by εἰς: 20:21; 24:24; 26:18. Acts 3:16c finds a parallel only in 1 Pet. 1:21, τοὺς δι' αὐτοῦ πιστούς.

[124] Luke ordinarily uses ἐνώπιον for "in the presence of." The only other use of ἀπέναντι is in Acts 17:7, where it expresses the notion of opposition.

90

name of Jesus nor faith in the name is mentioned again until the short address of Acts 4. No active role in the salvation of the hearers is indicated by this verse.

II. *Jesus as eschatological prophet.* The earthly ministry of Jesus is interpreted in terms of the eschatological prophet awaited in late Judaism:[125]

   A. Jesus was regarded as a prophet during his lifetime. While certain sayings may be editorial additions of the evangelists,[126] the opinion of the people of Mark 6:15 is probably an authentic reference. Besides, as Hahn has pointed out, the demand for a sign is well attested in the tradition;[127] and one does not ask a rabbi for a sign, but a prophet. Given the primitive self-understanding of the community as the congregation of the end of days,[128] no interpretation of the ministry of Jesus lay more readily at hand than that of the eschatological prophet.

   B. The extended Moses typology of the primitive traditions used in the composition of Acts 3 and 7 points to the understanding of Jesus as eschatological prophet.

   C. The expression χρόνων ἀποκαταστάσεως, as was noted above, indicates the use of Elijah typology.[129] That Jesus was regarded as Elijah by some people during his lifetime seems probable (Mark 6:15). That the early community should describe his ministry in terms of the Elijah mission of preparation of the people for the eschatological intervention of God seems reasonable.

III. *Jesus as messiah.* The life of Jesus, as far as it is reflected in the synoptic traditions, was not messianic measured by traditional messianic ideas.[130] Not only did Jesus probably never use the title messiah of himself,[131] he probably rejected it and what it implied.[132] Ironically it was as a "messianic" disturber of the

---

[125] Hahn, *Hoheitstitel*, 351-404, argues that this was an early understanding of the role of Jesus which has left traces in the gospel traditions. See Fuller, *Foundations*, 46-49.

[126] Matt. 21:11, 46; Luke 7:16; 24:19; John 6:4; 7:40.

[127] Both Mark (8:11f.) and Q (Luke 11:29), and the Johannine traditions (6:30).

[128] R. Bultmann, *Theology of the New Testament* 1, trans. Kendrick Grobel (New York: Scribner's, 1951), 37.

[129] Teeple, *Prophet*, 3-9.

[130] Bultmann, *Theology* 1, 27.

[131] E. Stauffer, "Messias oder Menschensohn," *NovT* 1 (1956), 81-102.

[132] Hahn, *Hoheitstitel*, 161-73.

peace that he was put to death by the Romans. It would seem strange that the primitive community should choose to designate Jesus as the messiah.

Yet the title attained widespread use so early that already in Antioch members of the community are said to have been called Χριστιανοί (Acts 11:26),[133] and by the time of Paul 'Iησοῦς Χριστός had already become a proper name (see n. 26). How is the use of the title for Jesus to be explained?

As Bultmann has pointed out,[134] the earliest community was an eschatological sect within Judaism, a congregation that regarded itself as the chosen recipient of the salvation promised by God for the end time. The decisive event by which this salvation was made known was the coming of Jesus. Hence the designation and proclamation of Jesus as the messiah, the bringer of salvation,[135] is implied in the very existence of the community.[136]

IV. *Jesus' role at the end time.* The primitive community breathed apocalyptic expectation; its attention was totally directed to the imminent and final intervention of God. Hence, titles were assigned to Jesus in function of his return at the end time. S. Schulz has argued that the earliest designation of Jesus as "lord" occurs in the *mar*-sayings, which point to his role in the coming judgment.[137] The son of Man sayings which attribute an eschatological function to Jesus by this title are almost certainly due to the Aramaic-speaking community.[138] Hence Bultmann's contention

[133] Haenchen, *Apostelgeschichte*, 311*f*.

[134] Bultmann, *Theology* 1, 42*f*. See Richard Zehnle, *The Making of the Christian Church* (Notre Dame, Ind.: Fides, 1969), 13-55.

[135] H. Conzelmann, *Grundriss der Theologie des Neuen Testaments* (München: Kaiser, 1967), 92. [English trans. by J. Bowden, *An Outline of the Theology of the New Testament* (New York: Harper & Row, 1969).]

[136] See J. H. Hayes, "The Resurrection as Enthronement and the Earliest Church Christology," *Interpretation* 22 (1968), 333-45; S. E. Johnson, "The Davidic-Royal Motif in the Gospels," *JBL* 87 (1968), 136-50.

[137] S. Schulz, "Maranatha und Kyrios Jesus," *ZNW* 53 (1962), 125-44.

[138] Thus H. E. Tödt, *The Son of Man in the Synoptic Tradition*, trans. D. Barton (Philadelphia: Westminster Press, 1965), follows Bultmann in tracing sayings about the future son of Man to Jesus, while denying that he identified himself with this son of Man. The identification would have been made by the early community. P. Vielhauer, "Jesus und der Menschensohn," *ZTK* 60 (1963), 133-77, argues that none of the sayings are authentic, as does Norman Perrin, *Rediscovering the Teaching of Jesus* (New York: Harper, 1967), 164-99. However, both agree that the future sayings are the earliest, and are to be attributed to the Palestinian community. Eduard Schweizer, "Der Menschensohn," *ZNW* 50 (1959), 185-209;

is correct, that "when Jesus was proclaimed as messiah it was *as the coming Messiah.*" [139] The messiahship of Jesus formed part of the eschatological expectation of the most primitive community, which is exactly the picture of Acts 3:20*f.*

E. Haenchen has objected that Acts 3:21 introduces the idea of the delay of the parousia, and hence must be reckoned as late.[140] E. Schweizer notes that "πρῶτον (3:26) at least is only possible at a time where [*sic*] the mission to the heathen was already going on." [141] To these claims it must be replied:

1. To say that 3:21 introduces the idea of the "delay of the parousia" is to play with words. As Peter speaks Jesus is in heaven; the parousia (obviously!) has not yet happened. This verse hardly entails the later Christian awareness of the delay of the parousia, especially embedded as it is in an appeal to Jews to hasten the return of Jesus by heeding his message of repentance.

2. As it stands in 3:26, πρῶτον may well modify ἀναστήσας, which would then denote the earthly mission of Jesus as his first sending by God, with his second (3:22 ἀποστείλῃ) to take place at the end time. To this correspond the first and second sendings of the brethren to Joseph in Stephen's speech: 7:12 ἐξαπέστειλεν . . . πρῶτον; 7:13 ἐν τῷ δευτέρῳ. It is only in the second sending that Joseph is recognized by his brethren! [142]

That the possibility of Schweizer's interpretation of πρῶτον suggested itself to Luke in his overall plan for Acts is not to be doubted (cf. 13:46). That much of the speech reflects the literary composition of Luke is rather obvious. But that the christological statement of 3:21 presupposes the delay of the parousia and is therefore to be ascribed to Luke and not to early tradition has not been proven.

V. *Jesus inactive in heaven.* The early community never assigned to

"Son of Man," *JBL* 79 (1960), 119-29; "The Son of Man Again," *NTS* 9 (1962/ 1963), 256-61, contends that the sayings which reflect the suffering and future exaltation of Jesus are authentic. But he too ascribes the future son of Man sayings to the early community.

[139] Bultmann, *Theology* 1, 33. According to Bultmann, this view of the messiah remains within the frame of Jewish eschatological expectation (33*f.*).

[140] Haenchen, *Apostelgeschichte*, 168.

[141] Eduard Schweizer, *Lordship and Discipleship*, SBT 28 (1960), 57*f.* n. 3.

[142] Cf. Bacon, "Speech," 248.

Jesus the role of the terrestrial messiah, the restoration of earthly rule of Israel. The first functions assigned were connected to the end time, and to the title son of Man. But the discourse of Acts 3, and especially the statement of 3:19-21, is singular in the New Testament in that it does not even assign a definite end time role to Jesus.[143] The future son of Man sayings depict Jesus as accuser (or defender) in the final judgment (Luke 12:8f.), or coming judge (Matt. 16:27), or bringer of the end time (Mark 13:26). What may be the earliest New Testament document, Paul's first letter to the Thessalonians,[144] reflects a doctrine of the coming of Jesus far more developed than that of Acts 3—Jesus will come gloriously accompanied by his saints (1 Thess. 3:13) to save those who have believed in him from the wrath of God (1:10) and to reward their fidelity (2:19).

The present relevance of Jesus according to Acts 3 lies in the continued proclamation of his message of repentance by his disciples. Though he is now in heaven awaiting the final intervention of God, his message still demands decision from the people to whom he was sent.

Conclusion. The discourse of Acts 3 is the most primitive and undeveloped christological statement in the New Testament.

Conclusion

An investigation of the thought content of the speeches of Acts 2 and 3 indicates that whereas the former constitutes a summary statement of the theological viewpoint of the author, the latter lacks essential elements of his usual position and presents unusual features, whose most logical explanation is the presence of primitive source material.

---

[143] In 1 Enoch 90:37 there is a vision of the new Jerusalem, and a white bull, a symbol for the messiah, is born in it. R. H. Charles, *The Book of Enoch* (Oxord: Clarendon Press, 1893), 222, notes that this is not the *prophetic* messiah "for he has absolutely no function to perform, as he does not appear until the world's history is finally closed."

[144] Cf. Werner G. Kümmel, *Introduction to the New Testament,* trans. A. J. Mattill, Jr. (Nashville: Abingdon Press, 1966), 182-87. Even if it be held that the epistle is not Paul's, or that some other epistle preceded it, the argument stands. For whichever letter of Paul be judged the earliest New Testament document, its teaching on the coming of Jesus will be seen to be more developed than that of Acts 3.

3. The Speeches in the Structure of Acts

An analysis of the literary composition and thought content of the discourse of Acts 2 indicates that Luke fashioned it as a solemn summary statement of his own theological viewpoint. On the contrary, Acts 3, on the basis of both composition and content, suggests the presence of primitive traditions, recognized and used as such by the author. A study of the place of these discourses in the plan of the author, revealed through an analysis of the structure of the book of Acts, confirms the conclusions reached in the previous chapters.

The Discourse of Acts 2: Keynote Address

Acts 1:1–2:42 (or for convenience' sake, Acts 1–2) is a careful statement by Luke of the ultimate reality underlying the mission or the "acts" of the apostles, which enables the reader to understand the material that follows. Literary analysis reveals that the four pericopes that compose this section constitute a unit in Luke's mind, to which reference is made at key moments in Acts.

Acts 1:1-14. Résumé and Introduction

In the opening statement of Acts, Luke informs us of the continuity of this work with the first book he has written for Theophilus, a book now known as the gospel of Luke (or the third gospel). He begins this second volume by relating the leave-taking of Jesus from his disciples, which he had previously narrated in Luke 24:36-53.[1] A

---

[1] P. Menoud, "Remarques sur les textes de l'ascension dans Luc-Actes," *Neutestamentliche Studien für R. Bultmann,* 148-56, defends the thesis that Luke-Acts was originally one volume, which was divided into two at the time of its introduction into the canon by the addition of Luke 24:50-53 and Acts 1:1-5. This suggestion has not found wide acceptance among exegetes. It is specifically answered by Jacques Dupont, " 'ΑΝΕΛΗΜΦΘΗ (Acts 1:2)," *NTS* 8 (1961/1962), 154-57 and C. F. D. Moule, "The Ascension, Acts 1:9," *ExpT* 68 (1956/1957), 205-9. Haenchen, *Apostelgeschichte,* 88 n. 2, replies to Menoud, in addition to his detailed com-

study of the details in the two narratives reveals a change of perspective behind the retelling of the incident.

I. *The mission of the apostles.* A first series of changes regards the instruction given by Jesus to his disciples, and their inability to grasp it fully:

    A. The time of leave-taking. It is very difficult to avoid the impression from Luke 24 that Jesus is separated from his disciples (and borne into heaven) [2] on the day of the resurrection itself (see 24:1, 13, 33, 36). Yet in Acts 1:3 it is stated that Jesus was present to the apostles during forty days after his passion, giving them many convincing proofs and instructing them about the kingdom of God.

    That this forty-day period is to be understood as a later specification of time spent by the risen Christ with his disciples in Luke 24 is indicated by the participle συναλιζόμενος in 1:4. Lake and Cadbury[3] prefer interpreting this as an alternative spelling of συναυλιζόμενος which had come to mean "to pass the night," though they admit that only Eusebius and Augustine support this interpretation.[4] But συναλιζόμενος makes excellent sense, "to eat salt together with," and is attested in this meaning in early Christian literature.[5] Moreover the majority of versions

---

mentary on the passages in question, by two general arguments: (1) Acceptance into the canon was not accomplished by a single decision of church authorities who were then able to modify all copies of Luke-Acts in the same fashion, but it was a gradual process, and no traces of the hypothetical original text have been found. (2) It is part of Luke's own view of things that the life of Jesus was a distinct epoch in salvation-history, a conception which precludes his extending "the gospel" beyond the exaltation of Jesus into the period of the church.

  [2] P. Benoit, "L'Ascension," *RB* 56 (1949), 161-203, argues that the Western reading is to be rejected: "Or l'omission de ces mots litigieux s'explique plus aisément que leur addition. Car ils font difficulté en plaçant l'Ascension au soir de la Résurrection, en contradiction avec Actes 1:3-11" (189). H. Schlier, "Jesu Himmelfahrt nach den lukanischen Schriften," *Geist und Leben* 34 (1961), 94, points out that the *great joy* of Luke 24:52 is motivated by an understanding that the resurrection is now complete with Jesus' reigning in heaven. But textual evidence and critical arguments have been advanced for both sides of this difficult question. A solution of the problem is not necessary to the thesis developed in the text, for either reading may be explained by the contention that what Luke has indicated in summary fashion at the end of the first volume he has developed in detail at the beginning of his second volume.

  [3] Lake and Cadbury, *Beginnings* 4, 4f.

  [4] Only a few minuscules read συναυλιζόμενος. According to Benoit, "L'Ascension," 191 n. 3: "Quant à la correction en συναυλιζόμενος, elle est arbitraire et parfaitement inutile."

  [5] See the discussion in Haenchen, *Apostelgeschichte,* 110 n. 1: In Clem. Rec. 7.2

have thus rendered the word;[6] and in a later discourse Luke has Peter mention that the risen Jesus ate and drank with his disciples (10:41). Hence συναλιζόμενος probably refers to the scene described in Luke 24:42f.[7]

B. The instruction of the apostles. In Luke 24:44-46 Jesus opens the understanding of the eleven and those with them (24:33) to comprehend the scriptures, and thus see that what was foretold by Moses and the prophets and the psalms was fulfilled in him. In the Acts Jesus has been teaching the apostles for forty days about the kingdom of God.[8] As he is about to leave, those who have come with him ask if in this time he will restore the kingdom to Israel. This question is understandable enough in the light of Jewish eschatological expectation: (1) Jesus' resurrection had evidently taken place, and resurrection was traditionally a sign of the end time.[9] (2) The outpouring of the Spirit was promised for the immediate future (Acts 1:5), another sign of the end time.[10] (3) The expression, ἀποκαθίσταναι τὴν βασιλείαν, refers to the establishment of the eschatological reign of God.[11]

But certainly the question must have seemed strange to Luke's Gentile readers. After all was not the community, which had extended itself to all parts of the Greek world, a direct outcome of the life and death of Jesus? And had he not surely

---

and Clem. Hom. 13.4, the word refers to the evening meal, which there consists of bread and salt.

[6] Peshitto, Harclean Syriac, Bohairic, Armenian, Vulgate.

[7] Barrett, *Luke*, 55. J. G. Davies, "The Prefigurement of the Ascension in the Third Gospel," *JTS* 6 (1955), 229-33, finds a parallel to Acts 1:1-12 in Luke 9:1-34 (the transfiguration). He claims that συναλιζόμενος corresponds to 9:10-17, the feeding of the five thousand. In his book, *He Ascended into Heaven. A Study in the History of Doctrine* (New York: Lutterworth, 1958), 52f., he contends that 1 Kings 19:8 (Elijah) is a typological basis for the ascension scene. Of Elijah it is said: καὶ ἔφαγεν καὶ ἔπιεν, which Davies relates to Acts 1:4; 10:41; Luke 24:43.

[8] P. Menoud, "La Pentecôte lucannienne et l'histoire," *RHPhilRel* 42 (1962), 142-47, notes that in rabbinic tradition repeating his teaching forty times means that a teacher has transmitted all his knowledge to his pupil, who may then teach in his turn (143).

[9] Lane, *Times of Refreshment*, 135.

[10] Alfred Wikenhauser, "Die Belehrung der Apostel durch den Auferstandenen nach Apg 1:3," *Vom Wort des Lebens. Festschrift Max Meinertz*, Neutestamentliche Abhandlungen, Ergänzungsband 1 (Münster, Westf.: Aschendorff, 1951), 109, sees a connection between Acts 1:6 and 2:17. The promise of the Spirit is understood as a sign of the end, the days of the messiah.

[11] Mal. 4:4f.; cf. Sir. 48:10: καταστῆσαι φυλὰς 'Ιακώβ (of Elijah).

known in advance what effect his mission would produce? And had he not communicated something of this plan to the disciples during the forty days of instruction? [12]

The answer of Jesus is moreover a mild rebuke. In 1:7 (note the adversative δέ) he reproves their concern with apocalyptic speculation about "times and seasons." And in 1:8 he announces a mission that is to go far beyond Israel, though in ambiguous terms, as will be seen below.

Luke was surely too careful an author not to realize this natural reaction of his Gentile readers to what he nevertheless knew was a normal reaction of Jewish disciples of Jesus. Later developments in Acts reveal only a gradual lifting of this "vincible ignorance" with the growing awareness that the gospel is to be preached to others besides the Jews. The author seems to be preparing his readers for the tension that will follow regarding the universality of the apostolic mission.

C. The final command of Jesus. In Luke 24 the final command of Jesus contains three specific elements:

1. 24:47 The disciples will preach repentance for the forgiveness of sins in the name of Jesus to all nations, beginning from Jerusalem.
2. 24:48 They will be witnesses of "these things."
3. 24:49 They must remain in the city until they are clothed with power from on high, the sending of the promise of the Father upon them.

These same three elements are present in the last words of Jesus to his apostles in the Acts, only in reverse order.

1. 1:4 The apostles are not to depart from Jerusalem, but are to await the promise of the Father "which you have heard from me." The following verse adds the specification, not in the gospel, that they will be "baptized" in the Holy Spirit.

---

[12] Wikenhauser, "Belehrung," 107, points out that in Acts βασιλεία never means "church." But it is certainly an oversubtlety to conclude that Luke's readers would therefore not be surprised at the disciples' failure to grasp the true nature of the apostolic mission after forty days' instruction by Jesus. Ernst Haenchen, "Judentum und Christentum in der Apostelgeschichte," ZNW 54 (1963), 155-87, argued that anyone who takes the forty days' teaching about the kingdom of God of Acts 1:3 seriously, must, in the light of 1:6, regard either the apostles as supremely stupid or Jesus as a poor teacher. This is perhaps an overstatement, but his subsequent position that the question does not depict the lack of understanding of the disciples (Apostelgeschichte, 111) accepts an either/or situation that does not do justice to the literary ability of Luke.

And Acts 1:8 takes up the word δύναμις of Luke 24:49, but specifies that it is the power of the Holy Spirit coming upon them.

2. 1:8 They will be witnesses "of me."

3. 1:8 "In Jerusalem and in all Judea and Samaria and to the end of the earth."

The final command in Acts specifically mentions the Holy Spirit, and outlines in greater detail the missionary program of the apostles. Regarding this program certain details merit closer consideration:

a. There is no mention of πάντα τὰ ἔθνη as in Luke 24:47. It is not until after the Cornelius incident that ἔθνη occurs in the sense of Gentiles actually involved in the apostolic mission, when Peter must defend his actions in Jerusalem (Acts 11:1). The wording of the command of Jesus is deliberately left inexplicit regarding the Gentiles, which allows for the gradually developing awareness in the community that its mission is to all men.[13]

b. The plan of Acts follows 1:8. The first five chapters deal with the community in Jerusalem. The death of Stephen prepares the way for preaching in the region of Judea and Samaria (8:1). The mission ἕως ἐσχάτου τῆς γῆς is announced by Paul in 13:47, and the rest of Acts becomes the story of Paul's carrying the message all the way to Rome, where he declares that salvation has been sent to the ἔθνεσιν (28:28).[14] When Paul gives an outline of his work to Agrippa (26:20) he mentions simply: Damascus, Jerusalem, all of Judea (which is unusual in the light of Gal. 1:22, and betrays the theological purpose of the author), and τοῖς ἔθνεσιν. But Luke avoids mentioning the ἔθνη in Acts 1:8, which allows a rewording of Luke 24:47 more in harmony with the development of Acts.

[13] See E. Jacquier, *Les Actes des Apôtres*, Études Bibliques, 2nd ed. (Paris: Victor Lecoffre, 1926), 15f. Commentators have noted the reference to Isa. 49:4, and have pointed out that a reference to the Gentiles is thus implicit in 1:8. In the mind of Luke, 1:8 surely includes the Gentile mission, but omission of explicit mention of πάντα τὰ ἔθνη still allows it to be interpreted as a command to preach the message to Jews all over the world in the diaspora.

[14] J. Dupont, "Le salut des gentils et la signification théologique du Livre des Actes," *Études sur les Actes des Apôtres*, Lectio Divina 45 (Paris: Cerf, 1967), 393-419.

Conclusion. In Acts there is a greater insistence on the instruction of Jesus, but the disciples do not seem to grasp its implications for the mission they are to undertake. Specifically they do not understand that they are to preach the message of Jesus to the Gentiles, and this feature is deliberately left inexplicit in the command of Jesus that sets the program for their mission.[15]

II. *The ascension.* Another series of changes concerns the description of the leave-taking. In Luke 24:50-52 the departure is straightforward enough; in Acts, an ascension scene is described:

A. The place of the leave-taking. In Luke 24:50 Jesus leads his apostles "toward Bethany"; in Acts 1:12 they have been on the Mount of Olives, a sabbath's journey from Jerusalem. There is of course no geographical contradiction here, but a shift of emphasis, for a mountain is certainly a better location if one is to describe an ascension scene.

B. The two men. Where Luke 24:51 simply relates that Jesus parted from his disciples and was taken up into heaven, Acts 1:9-11 describes an ascension scene in which there are two men in white clothing, who recall not only the two men at the tomb on the day of the resurrection (24:5ff.), but also Moses and Elijah at the transfiguration (9:30).[16] Just as the two men of the resurrection story used a question to remind the women that what they were doing (seeking the living among the dead) was clearly not what Jesus wanted them to do according to what he had said in Galilee, so here by means of a question they indicate to the apostles that they are not to stand looking up into heaven.[17]

---

[15] See Johannes Munck, *The Acts of the Apostles,* revised by William F. Albright and C. S. Mann, The Anchor Bible 31 (New York: Doubleday, 1967), 8.

[16] According to M. D. Goulder, *Type and History in Acts* (London: SPCK, 1964), 147f., the two men of Acts 1:10 are not angels, but Moses and Elijah, both of whom were believed to have ascended into heaven. The Moses type explains why Jesus taught his apostles for forty days and about the kingdom. Elijah was taken to heaven before the sending of the spirit upon Elisha. Manek, "New Exodus," 11, notes that only Luke 9:30 refers to Moses and Elijah as ἄνδρες δύο in the transfiguration scene (cf. Mark 9:4; Matt. 17:3). Similarly only Luke 24:4 has ἄνδρες δύο at the tomb after the resurrection (Mark 16:5: νεανίσκον; John 20:12: δύο ἀγγέλους).

[17] For P. A. van Stempvoort, "The Interpretation of the Ascension in Luke and Acts," *NTS* 5 (1958/1959), 30-42, Luke 24:50-53 is a "doxological" interpretation of the ascension. In a scene that recalls Sir. 50:20-22, the gospel ends with Jesus as

C. The cloud. For Luke the ascension is a prefiguration of the return of Jesus, who will return in the manner in which he has gone to heaven. The νεφέλη of v. 9 is an echo of Luke 21:27, where the singular (cloud) describes the coming of the son of Man, a change from the plural of Mark 13:26.[18]

D. ἀνελήμφθη. The key to the meaning of the ascension scene in Acts is given by the word ἀνελήμφθη. The passive aorist of ἀναλαμβάνειν, which seems to have become a technical term for the assumption of the blessed into heaven at this time,[19] occurs only five times in the New Testament. 1 Tim. 3:16, undoubtedly a Christian hymn dating from a time when Christianity had already begun to be diffused throughout the Greco-Roman world (ἐκηρύχθη ἐν ἔθνεσιν), makes six statements about Jesus, all in the same literary form, the last of which is ἀνελήμφθη ἐν δόξῃ. Neither the resurrection nor the ascension of Jesus is referred to; evidently the entire "taking up" of Jesus into glory is seen as a unit.[20]

Three of the other four uses of ἀνελήμφθη occur in the first chapter of Acts to refer to the ascension of Jesus (1:2, 11, 22),[21] which concludes a theme begun earlier in the third gospel. When Moses and Elijah appear with Jesus at the transfiguration (9:30f.) they are speaking of the ἔξοδος he is about to make in Jerusalem. Shortly after, the journey to Jerusalem begins (9:51), which evidently marks one of the major divisions of the gospel, and Luke announces that the time has come for the ἀνάλημψις of Jesus to be fulfilled. This noun, which occurs nowhere else in the New Testament but is found in other places in the contemporary literature to denote the assumption

---

"blessing priest." "It is a glorious but a limited interpretation, for history goes on and the Church cannot remain in the attitude of the προσκυνῆσις and the εὐλογία" (37). The "inner circle" must go outside into the world. Hence, Acts 1:9-11 gives a totally different interpretation. "We might refer to it as the ecclesiastical and historical interpretation, with the accent on the work of the Spirit in the Church" (39). It is hard and realistic, ordered to a mission; "the barren contemplation of the mirabilia is rejected" (39).

[18] J. A. T. Robinson, *Jesus*, 132 n. 2.

[19] A. Plummer, *A Critical and Exegetical Commentary on the Gospel according to St. Luke*, The International Critical Commentary (Edinburgh: Clark, 1896), 262.

[20] Cf. G. Bertram, "Die Himmelfahrt Jesu vom Kreuz aus und der Glaube an seine Auferstehung," *Festgabe für A. Deissmann* (Tübingen: Mohr, 1927), 187-217.

[21] The fifth use refers to the taking up of the vision from Peter in Joppa (Acts 10:16).

of the blessed into heaven,[22] is evidently chosen for its relation to ἀνελήμφθη. Acts offers a graphic representation of the completion of the last stich of 1 Tim. 3:16—"He was taken up in glory." The ἀνάλημψις of Jesus, his death-resurrection-ascension, which began in Luke 9:51, is now consummated.[23]

This interpretation is confirmed by the Lukan description of the actual departure of Jesus as "going on his way" (1:11, 12 πορεύεσθαι). This verb is thematic in the gospel denoting the foreordained going-on-his-way of Jesus to the cross.[24] With the ascension the "going" of Jesus is completed.

Conclusion. For Luke the complete story of Jesus and his continuing relevance in the world was not told in the third gospel. He has left the consummation of the ἀνάλημψις for the retelling of the leave-taking which opens the second volume of his work, for reasons which will be apparent later on.[25]

III. *Expectation.* The most significant series of changes is that by which a note of immediate expectation has been injected into the scene of the leave-taking of Jesus in Acts 1:

A. The logion of John Baptist. Luke 3:16f. points to one who will accomplish the eschatological purification and judgment in wind and fire,[26] namely to the messiah. An original logion has probably been given a Christian interpretation by the addition of ἁγίῳ to πνεύματι in the Q-source (Luke 3:16; Matt. 3:11). Further changes are made when Jesus recalls the logion in Acts 1:5:

1. In Acts there is no mention of fire. There will be fire (and wind) in the event itself, but at the moment the author is more interested in placing the accent on the Spirit, the Holy Spirit he has just mentioned (1:2). Thus the logion is given a decisively Christian interpretation.

2. In Luke 3:16 it is the one coming who will baptize; in Acts the verb βαπτισθήσεσθε is the passive voice. This is not a con-

[22] Plummer, *Luke*, 262.

[23] Dupont, " 'ΑΝΕΛΗΜΦΘΗ," refutes van Stempvoort's claim that ἀνελήμφθη refers only to the death of Jesus.

[24] Cf. n. 27 of the preceding chapter. The verb is not found in the leave-taking of Luke 24.

[25] Barrett, *Luke*, 56f.

[26] P. van Imschoot, "Baptême d'eau et baptême d'Esprit Saint," *ETL* 13 (1936), 653-66.

tradiction, for John Baptist is not explicit as to how the one coming will baptize, and Luke certainly depicts the coming "baptism" as effected by Jesus (who pours out the Spirit according to 2:33). But the passive voice is a clearer reference to the event for which the reader is being prepared.

3. The addition in Acts of "not many days hence" prepares the reader for the event at Pentecost. No matter what the significance of the number forty on a deeper level, the reader will, by a simple arithmetic calculation, recognize the Pentecost event as the fulfillment of the prophecy of Jesus.

Before the mission of Jesus, John Baptist referred to the coming of the stronger one, who would accomplish the eschatological purification and judgment. The risen Jesus now foretells the imminent fulfillment of John's words through a "baptism" in the Holy Spirit.

B. The subsequent activity of the disciples. Luke 24:53 brings the third gospel to a solemn conclusion: The eleven and those with them are praising God with great joy in the temple. In Acts 1:12 the same group returns to Jerusalem (ὑπέστρεψαν εἰς Ἰερουσαλήμ as in Luke 24:53), but they do not go to the temple. Leaving the Mount of Olives (which would seem to be the editing of Luke: compare Luke 22:39 and Mark 14:32), they enter the city and ascend to the ὑπερῷον, which refers to a private house and recalls that private house in which Jesus had his last supper with his disciples. There the disciples remain and persevere in prayer, a characteristic preface to important events in Luke-Acts, which serves to heighten the note of expectation already introduced by the parting words of Jesus.[27]

Conclusion. Clearly something important is about to happen, and that something has to do with the Holy Spirit who is mentioned three times in the first eight verses of Acts.

IV. *Synthesis.* In the retelling of the leave-taking of Jesus in Acts, Luke has introduced a three-fold change of perspective:[28]

A. The kingdom. The apostles have not grasped the full implica-

[27] Thus in the third gospel Jesus prays before the descent of the Spirit (3:21), the call of the 12 (6:12), the confession of Peter (9:18), the transfiguration (9:28) and the passion (22:40). Only in the last-mentioned instance do Matthew and Mark have a similar reference. The practice is continued in the Acts. See 1:24; 6:6; 8:15; 9:11, 40; 10:9, 30; 11:5; 12:12; 13:3; 28:8 (cf. 14:23; 16:25; 20:36; 21:5).

[28] Cf. Benoit, "L'Ascension," 190f.

tions of Jesus' teaching about the universal nature of the kingdom, even though he has taught them about the kingdom during a significant period of time since the resurrection.

B. The ἀνάλημψις. There can now be no doubt that the earthly mission of Jesus is over; the ἀνάλημψις of Luke 9:51 has clearly been accomplished.

C. The Spirit. The reader is prepared for a significant intervention of the Holy Spirit in the immediate future.[29]

Acts 1:15-26. The Selection of Matthias

The expectation of the reader is not to be fulfilled immediately, for at this point Luke narrates an episode which seems to contribute little to the course of events—the selection of Matthias as successor to Judas in order to fill up the number of the twelve apostles.

I. *Provenance of the pericope.* At first glance the episode presents itself as an example of early tradition which Luke has simply incorporated into his narrative. On closer inspection evidences of Lukan editing abound:

A. Vocabulary and style. In an exhaustive study of the vocabulary of this pericope, J. Renié[30] has estimated that 72% (41 of 56 words) of the significant words bear the stamp of Luke. Features of Lukan style are so abundant that Renié concludes that if the vocabulary alone already betrays the hand of Luke, the style exhibits it even more (53).

B. Structure.[31] Luke has structured the pericope around the double citation of scripture in 1:20. The first part of Peter's address (1:16-19) shows the scriptural necessity of the past event of the demise of Judas (ἔδει is the first word after the salutation); it is explained by 1:20a (Ps. 69:25). The second part (1:21f.) declares the necessity of choosing a successor (1:21 begins δεῖ); it comments on 1:20b (Ps. 109:8). Scriptural text and fulfillment are arranged in chiastic order; past first, then present.

---

[29] According to C. F. Sleeper, "Pentecost and Resurrection," *JBL* 84 (1965), 389-99, the last two are related: "The period of the appearances is that of the promise of the Spirit, and the ascension narrative has such an important place in Acts because it makes possible the fulfillment of that promise" (391f.)

[30] J. Renié, "L'élection de Matthias (Actes 1:15-26). Authenticité du récit," *RB* 55 (1948), 43-53.

[31] J. Dupont, "La destinée de Judas prophétisée par David," *Études,* 309-20.

C. Continuance of themes. The three themes detected in the first pericope have been continued in this narrative:

1. The Holy Spirit. The Holy Spirit is mentioned and in a rather unusual way. Peter (1:16) declares that "the Holy Spirit foretold through the mouth of David" the lot of Judas. This manner of citing a prophetical passage is rare in the New Testament. In the synoptic gospels something of this sort is found in the mouth of Jesus only in the Markan account of the discussion about David's son, "David himself said in the Holy Spirit" (Mark 12:36), where the reference is clearly to the spirit of Yahweh that bestowed the power of prophecy on the great figures of the Old Testament (cf. 2 Sam. 23:2).[32] No fulfillment text in the gospels specifically mentions the intervention of the Spirit.

In Acts the usual formula is "David says" or an equivalent phrase (2:16, 25, 31, 34; 3:22; 7:49), or "it is written" (7:42; 13:33, 40; 15:15). The Spirit is directly referred to only in 4:25, a solemn liturgical prayer of the community; 28:25, the tragic final words of Paul to the Jews in which he sees their rejection of Jesus as foretold in Isaiah; and 1:16. This unusual reference emphasizes the working of the Holy Spirit in the people of God and corresponds to the insistence on the role of the Spirit noted in 1:1-14.[33]

2. ἀνελήμφθη. The reader is reminded that the mission of Jesus has definitely ended by the repetition of the key word of the narrative of 1:1-14.

3. The lack of understanding by the apostles of the mission that was to be theirs will be discussed below.

D. Other Lukan themes

1. Witness. That the twelve were witnesses defines their principal function in Acts. Jesus assigns this role in 1:8, and Peter frequently recalls the fact that the apostles are witnesses, especially in 10:39 and 41 where he explains that the apparitions of Jesus were not for all the λαός but only for the foreordained witnesses. Even Paul declares that those who came up from

---

[32] Matthew reads simply "David in spirit calls him Lord" (22:43), and Luke: "For David himself says in the book of Psalms" (20:42).

[33] K. Rengstorf, "Die Zuwahl des Matthias," *ST* 16 (1962), 35-67, regards the manner of citing David in 1:16 as a sign that the Holy Spirit is in charge even in this waiting period.

Galilee with Jesus were later witnesses to him in Jerusalem (13:31).

2. Prayer. As noted above, prayer before an important action (1:24f.) is typically Lukan (see n. 27).

3. The scriptural citation. Whatever the source of the passage quoted, the mention of the "book of Psalms" is exclusively Lukan; only he of the New Testament writers mentions the canonical psalms as a book (Luke 20:42; 24:44; Acts 1:20; 13:33).

E. Place of the pericope. There is no indication that Luke had exact knowledge of the time at which this incident actually occurred;[34] ἐν ταῖς ἡμέραις ταύταις is a common Lukan introduction (Luke 1:39; 2:1; 6:12; Acts 6:1; 12:27). The choice of a place for the pericope seems inexplicable at first reading, since Jesus neither replaced Judas himself during the forty days nor left orders for Peter to do so (at least Peter does not claim to be fulfilling a command of Jesus).[35]

F. Indications of a source. The fate of Judas (1:18), the name of his burial place (1:19),[36] the scriptural citations (1:20), and the names of the candidates (1:23) could have come to Luke from early traditions. But the composition of the narrative and, as will be shown, its place in the development come from Luke himself.

Conclusion. The preponderance of Lukan elements and themes point to the author of Luke-Acts as chiefly responsible for the narrative of 1:15-26, though some of the details undoubtedly reflect early traditions.

II. Meaning of the pericope. The place of this narrative in Acts can be appreciated only in the context of the forward movement of the author's plan:

A. Negative explanation. The incident demonstrates graphically one of the three themes noted in the analysis of 1:1-14—the

---

[34] Reicke, Glaube, 22.

[35] It is precisely on this basis that Dupont, Problèmes, 81, remarks that Renié should have brought up the question of sources. But it will be shown that the pericope fits quite well into its present setting according to the plan of Luke.

[36] Pierre Benoit, "La Mort de Judas," Synoptische Studien. Festschrift A. Wikenhauser (München: Zink, 1953), 1-19, holds that the two accounts of the death of Judas (Acts 1:15-26 and Matt. 27:3-10) show the influence of a popular story which conserved the name of the place of his burial.

failure of the apostles to comprehend the mission that had been confided to them.

1. Matthias and the twelve. Matthias is never again heard of in the Acts, and the twelve have only a minor role in the total missionary effort. They are named in 1:13; Peter and the eleven are mentioned in 2:14; and the twelve appear in 6:2 when they take the initiative in appointing the seven. Otherwise they are given the less restrictive title "apostles," and in this capacity they form a chorus for the acts of Peter, or general statements are made about their activity. After 16:4 nothing more is heard of them.

Individual members of the twelve fare little better. John is mentioned nine times, usually as accompanying Peter, and never as an independent agent (3:1, 3, 4, 11; 4:13, 19; 8:14; cf. 1:13; 12:2). James, John's brother, is mentioned only in 12:2, which recounts his martyrdom.[37] Only Peter plays an important role in Acts, but except for a brief mention in 15:7-11 and 14, his address in the council at Jerusalem, it is confined to the first twelve chapters.

Luke has prepared the reader for such a development in his gospel. Only he has a second sending out of disciples by Jesus after that of the twelve. Numerous elements in the second sending indicate that a universal mission is being foreshadowed, and significantly it is not the twelve who are commissioned, but seventy other disciples.[38] The twelve are always closely connected with the preaching to Israel. In the last supper scene Luke has Jesus declare to the apostles that in his kingdom they will sit on thrones judging the twelve tribes of Israel (Luke 22:30). Thus the martyrdom of James (Acts 12:2) required no replacement in the ranks of the twelve; but the crime and suicide of Judas disqualified him for the role of the twelve in the kingdom.[39]

2. The choice of missionaries. It has been held that the purpose of the pericope is to give the meaning of the title "apostle"

---

[37] James of Jerusalem is not to be identified with the other James of the list of the 12. The latter is clearly identified as Ἰάκωβος Ἀλφαίου in 1:13, an appellation never accorded to the leader of the Jerusalem community (Acts 12:17; 15:13; 21:18).

[38] W. Grundmann, *Das Evangelium nach Lukas,* 2nd ed. (Berlin: Evangelische Verlagsanstalt, 1961); Theologisches Handkommentar zum Neuen Testament 16, 207.

[39] Jackson and Lake, *Beginnings* 1, 298*f.* Cf. P. Menoud, "Les additions au groupe des douze apôtres, d'après le livre des Actes," *RHPhilRel* 37 (1957), 75.

as one who had not only witnessed the resurrection, but also the public life of Jesus from the beginning. That this concept is here attributed to Peter and the primitive community is obvious.[40] But for Luke the Spirit is free to choose apostles without reference to the rule of 1:21f. Thus Paul does not fulfill Peter's qualifications, but not only is he an apostle (with Barnabas: 14:4, 14), he is also qualified as a witness by an apparition of Jesus (26:16).

Evidently the approval of the visible community is needed for apostolic work. Stephen and the other six enter into their functions only after the apostles have imposed hands upon them (6:6). Peter and John are sent from Jerusalem to approve Philip's activity in Samaria (8:14), and Barnabas is sent on a similar mission to Antioch (11:22). It seems strange that the brilliant Apollos should need the instruction of Priscilla and Aquila (18:26), yet in this way he is brought into harmony with the community (Priscilla and Aquila have been presented as co-workers and fellow travelers of Paul),[41] and his mission to Corinth receives its approval (18:27).

But without the intervention of the Spirit no apostolate is possible. Even the reconstituted twelve must obey the command of Jesus to remain in Jerusalem until they have received the power of the Holy Spirit and can begin their mission.[42] For Paul there is no conflict: His first mission is from both the Holy Spirit (13:2) and the community (13:3), and the way

---

[40] For M. Goguel, "La conception jérusalémite de l'Église et les phénomènes de pneumatisme," *Mélanges Franz Cumont*, Annuaire de l'Institut de Philologie et d'Histoire Orientales et Slaves 4 (Brussels: Secrétariat de l'Institut, 1936), 211-23, there are evidences of two different conceptions of the apostolate in early Christianity: the Pauline, which was charismatic, and the Jerusalem, which was institutional. He sees the Pauline as having been formulated earlier; the latter arose when the former disappeared and the preponderant role of the early apostles became fundamental to the notion.

[41] E. Käsemann, "The Disciples of John the Baptist in Ephesus," *Essays*, 147.

[42] M. Goguel, "Pneumatisme et eschatologie dans le christianisme primitif," *Revue de l'Histoire des Religions* 132 (1946), 124-69, and 133 (1947/1948), 103-61, notes the difference: "Les Douze n'ont pas tenu leur autorité d'un don de l'Esprit, mais des instructions qu'ils avaient reçues du Seigneur pendant son ministère et de la mission que, tacitement ou implicitement, il leur avait confiée. Leur autorité est donc fondée dans le passé; elle ne dérive pas d'une action présente du Christ ou de l'Esprit. Les Douze ne sont pas apôtres parce qu'ils ont reçu l'Esprit, mais ils ont reçu l'Esprit parce qu'ils étaient apôtres" (2nd article, 123).

is cleared for his further work by a decision of the entire church in Jerusalem, which is at the same time attributed to the Holy Spirit (15:28).

Throughout the book of Acts Luke demonstrates that the leaders of the new community were not always equal of themselves to the mission that would be required of them, but needed the special intervention of the Spirit at key moments. Such a moment has arrived at this point in the narrative. Do they elect Matthias? His name is never heard again. Do they restore the twelve? They will have only a minor role subsequently. The mission given by Jesus is not to be accomplished according to the notions they have fashioned for themselves; it is the Spirit who will guide and lead them to understand the truth.

Negatively, then, this pericope continues one of the three special themes noted in the retelling of the leave-taking of Jesus, namely the failure of the apostles to grasp the full implication of his teaching on the kingdom, and specifically the fact that the kingdom was to be preached to all men and not only to Israel.[43]

B. Positive explanation.[44] An analysis of the positive thrust of this narrative exposes more clearly its present form and place in the Acts.

1. Past. Acts 1:21f. summarizes Luke's ἀνάλημψις theme: A witness is one who has seen all that Jesus did of salvific significance. The period of his activity is neatly circumscribed by the baptism of John and his taking up into heaven. The great period of the mission of Jesus on earth has ended; there is nothing more to witness.

2. Present. The pericope indicates much about the self-consciousness of the group gathered in the upper room. According to 1:15b, "the group of persons assembled together was about 120." This seemingly useless (and hardly prepared by 1:13f.) bit of information is awkwardly inserted between "Peter said" and his actual words. The number 120 is not just a fortuitous choice of a multiple of twelve.[45] In rabbinic tradition the members of the great synagogue, which sup-

---

[43] Rengstorf, "Zuwahl," 55.
[44] Ibid., 58-61.
[45] Reicke, Glaube, 23. Cf. S-B 2, 594f.

posedly ruled Judaism from Ezra until Simon the Just, numbered 120, a number reached by rightly or wrongly adding up the names found in Ezra 8–10. There was an opinion current at the time that 120 persons were required to make up an officially recognized synagogue. While the author may or may not intend to gather together a new "great synagogue" for the event that will follow, he has at least strengthened the juridical value of the decision made in 1:26. The group is conscious that it forms a special community in itself. Moreover it is clear that in this community a definite subgroup holds authority, namely, the twelve. And Peter evidently has the role of head of the entire community.

3. Future. The role played by Peter in the election of Matthias signals the role he will play in the beginning of the mission of the community. In the first twelve chapters of Acts there is only one discourse of any appreciable length given by anyone but Peter. He represents the twelve before the sanhedrin; the visitation of the new communities devolves upon him (9: 31*f.*) ; he personally makes the breakthrough in accepting Gentiles into the community; and his argument changes the murmurings of certain members of the Jerusalem church to praise of God (11:1-19). It is little wonder that when Herod Agrippa decides that the time is ripe to attack the new community, he chooses to strike against Peter (12:3).

The importance of the twelve, the group personally chosen by Jesus, also becomes evident in the beginning of the mission. Already on Pentecost when the first apostolic preaching is described and the later universal mission is foreshadowed the role of the twelve as a "college" is underlined: Only one can give the actual sermon, but Peter speaks in the name of all (2:14, 37, 42). Later the approval of the college (under the more general rubric of the "apostles") will be given to the important breakthroughs in the expanding mission: through Peter and John as delegates in Samaria (8:14) ; by consenting to the admission of Cornelius to the community (11:1, 18) ; by the decision of the "council" of Jerusalem. It is precisely because this college is the group that was chosen by Jesus to be with him and to share in his work that they can guarantee the continuity between his own mission and that of the church.

110

Thus, while something new is announced in 1:1-14, a coming intervention of the Spirit, this pericope assures that the community in which the Spirit is awaited is basically the same as the group that followed Jesus during his lifetime.[46] The twelve, reconstituted by the addition of one of the close followers of Jesus in the place of Judas, still has a privileged place, and Peter is spokesman and leader of the twelve.[47]

Conclusion. The primary intention of Luke in placing the election of Matthias in its present place would seem to be a desire to emphasize the continuity between the mission of Jesus which is now terminated by his ἀνάλημψις and the mission of the apostles which will begin when they have received the Holy Spirit in the near future. It is true that this mission will go far beyond the imperfect understanding of the apostles, and eventually others will be recruited to take on the burden of the work. But the role of the twelve is not repudiated; it is surpassed, but it remains as the link to the mission of Jesus himself.[48]

Acts 2:1-14a. The Pentecost Event

The expectation evoked by the final words of Jesus to his disciples is fulfilled by the descent of the Holy Spirit on the group gathered in the upper room on Pentecost.

I. *Difficulties to historicity.* That the event should have occurred as narrated by Luke is highly improbable.
  A. Crass notions of "play-by-play" reporting succumb to the slightest probing of the details:
    1. The form of baptism undoubtedly employed by the primitive community was baptism by immersion.[49] Immersing three thousand people in a single day is quite a trick anywhere. In

---

[46] Cf. Goguel, "Conception," 213.

[47] Luke more than the other evangelists has insisted on the preeminent role of Peter in the gospel. Only in Luke is Peter alone called first, and a miraculous catch of fish highlights the call (5:1-11). Only Luke among the synoptics has a second "call" (22:31-34).

[48] C. Masson, "La reconstitution du collège des Douze d'après Actes 1,15-26," *Revue de Théologie et de Philosophie* (1955), 193-201, notes that another reason for the author's use of this pericope is to show that God's plan for the salvation of Israel remains in force, despite the widespread infidelity that reached even one of the chosen twelve.

[49] The community's baptism probably was derived from the baptism of John, and may have been influenced by the proselyte baptism of Judaism. Both were by immersion.

PETER'S PENTECOST DISCOURSE

Jerusalem at the height of the dry season it would be nothing short of a miracle.

2. Pilate's well-documented fear of crowds eventually led to his recall to Rome.[50] The great noise (2:5) and the gathering of the crowd are hardly conceivable in Jerusalem on a great feast day without the intervention of the Roman soldiers.

3. Haenchen[51] observes that it is extremely difficult to be heard by three thousand people in the open air, without a public address system.

B. G. Kretschmar has pointed out that, while the celebration of the ascension of Jesus on the fortieth day after Easter cannot be attested to before the fourth century, there is documentary evidence for the existence of a feast celebrating the ascension on the fiftieth day after Easter until that century in the East Syrian and Palestinian church. The practice testifies to an ancient tradition independent of and differing from the account of the Acts.[52] Eventually the Acts tradition asserted itself, and the celebration of the "outpouring of the Spirit" on the fiftieth day after Easter became universal, while the ascension was relegated to the fortieth day.

In the light of this evidence it is improbable that some spectacular event did take place in Jerusalem on the feast of Pentecost; it is moreover questionable that Luke's narrative depends on an early Palestinian source as far as the date is concerned.

C. The cumulative evidence of the rest of early Christian literature renders improbable any spectacular intervention of the Spirit at all in the early days of the community. According to John 20:22 the Spirit was bestowed upon the disciples by Jesus himself on the evening of the resurrection. Paul's great insistence on the role of the Spirit in creating the unity of the members of the community makes his non-use of the event[53] difficult to understand, if it really was an event.[54]

[50] Josephus, *War* 2. (9.4) 175-77; *Antiq.* 18. (4.1f.) 85-89.
[51] Haenchen, *Apostelgeschichte,* 151.
[52] Kretschmar, "Himmelfahrt," 209-11. Cf. Moule, "Ascension," 206.
[53] S. MacLean Gilmour, "The Christophany to More Than Five Hundred Brethren," *JBL* 80 (1961), 248-52, and "Easter and Pentecost," *JBL* 81 (1962), 62-66, has argued that the appearance of Jesus to the five hundred brethren of 1 Cor. 15:6 lies behind the Lukan Pentecost story, and that Luke was the first to differentiate between Easter and Pentecost, i.e., between the awareness of the risen Christ and the consciousness of the Holy Spirit.
[54] Admittedly the appeal to Paul is an argument from silence. But not all such

II. *Provenance of the pericope.* Lukan style and vocabulary are evident in every verse of the pericope. The extent to which traditions of such an event lay before him may be more closely defined by an analysis of the features of the narrative:

A. The date. Various motives may be suggested for Luke's selection of Pentecost for the event of Acts 2:1-14*a:*

1. Pentecost was the first big feast after the death of Jesus, the first occasion on which crowds would be assured in Jerusalem to witness the spectacular event and hear the apostolic preaching.[55]

2. Pentecost seems to have been highly regarded as the great pilgrimage feast by Jews of the diaspora (cf. 1 Cor. 16:8). E. Lohse[56] points out that diaspora Jews celebrated the feast twice in order to be sure to have a common celebration with the Jews in Palestine.

3. The feast is of primary importance in the original form of the book of Jubilees, and is connected with the covenant between God and Israel and its renewal.[57] Since this work was of great importance in the Qumran community, which may indeed have produced it,[58] it may be concluded—and the conclusion is supported by other evidence[59]—that the covenant interpretation of the feast of Pentecost was popular at Qumran in the century preceding the Christian era.[60] Aware

---

arguments are to be brushed lightly aside. In this case the "silence" is stupendous. Paul describes the Christian's life in the Spirit glowingly in Rom. 8; indicates that a variety of talents flows from the one Spirit whom all have received in 1 Cor. 12; and insists that God sent the Spirit to Christians in the fullness of time in Gal. 4. Paul does not hesitate to mention the resurrection appearances; why should he not mention a "historical fact" like the visible outpouring of the Spirit described in Acts 2?

[55] Cf. A. Causse, "Le pélerinage à Jérusalem et la première Pentecôte," *RHPhilRel* 20 (1940), 120-41.

[56] E. Lohse, "πεντηκοστή," *TDNT* 6, 47.

[57] W. Wiesenberg, "The Jubilee of Jubilees," *Revue de Qumran* 3 (1961/1962), 3-40.

[58] Eissfeldt, *Introduction*, 607f.

[59] J. Milik, *Ten Years of Discovery in the Wilderness of Judea,* SBT 27 (1959), 117.

[60] The same importance may be indicated for the Therapeutae of Egypt, a group possibly related to the Qumran convenanters. According to F. H. Colson, Loeb Classical Library 9 (Cambridge: Harvard University Press, 1941), 152, 522f., the vague reference in Philo's *The Contemplative Life* 65 to feasts of the Therapeutae possibly on every fiftieth day may indicate that they regarded Pentecost as the chief feast.

of this tradition, Luke may have chosen the feast as an appropriate date for the beginning of the "true continuation" of Israel.

It is usually objected that the covenant interpretation of the feast of weeks in the Mishnah was accepted only after a period of discussion. In the time of Trajan the question was still being debated; only in the middle of the second century are there texts which clearly accept the interpretation.[61] However, an interpretation of a feast which is accepted in the middle of the second century certainly antedates the acceptance by a considerable length of time. Official acceptance presupposes a long period of partial acceptance in various communities. Luke may certainly have known the Sinai interpretation of the feast of weeks.[62]

Noack has extended the objection: the covenant interpretation, while favored by groups in Judaism such as Qumran, was not admitted by the Pharisees until long after the destruction of Jerusalem caused a restructuring of Judaism. The author of Acts, who seems well disposed to the Pharisees, would not have supported the covenant interpretation against them.[63]

The weaknesses of the argument are evident. In the first place, the author's pro-Pharisee sentiment must be proved. The incidents of 5:34-40 (Gamaliel's address) and 23:6-9 (Pharisee-Sadducee dispute at Paul's hearing) are intended to show that Christianity was not in opposition to the accepted doctrines of Judaism. Elsewhere Luke has Paul declare (to Agrippa 26:22f.) that the scriptures revered by the

[61] S-B 2, 601.

[62] Kretschmar, "Himmelfahrt," 226f., argues that the book of Jubilees is not innovating, but reproducing earlier traditions. He notes evidence in Chronicles, the work of the levitical circles that preceded Jubilees chronologically, for the covenant interpretation of the feast of weeks. Further he argues that the Jewish understanding of the feast of weeks as a covenant feast may have influenced the Christian celebration of the ascension on the fiftieth day after Easter, on the basis of iconography (see chap. 2 n. 62) and early Christian liturgical readings for the feast (which resemble those of the synagogue; 230). It may be that Luke was aware of this tradition; Acts 2:33 seems to indicate a connection between Jesus' ascension and the outpouring of the Spirit (cf. Eph. 4:8). If so, it is evident that he has transformed it to suit his own purpose.

[63] B. Noack, "The Day of Pentecost in Jubilees, Qumran and Acts," *Annual of the Swedish Theological Institute* 1 (1962), 73-95.

Jews point the way to the Christian message. An author partial to the Pharisees would hardly single out converted Pharisees as the cause of the trouble in 15:5. Secondly, does it follow from the fact that the Pharisees did not admit the covenant interpretation of Pentecost until long after the destruction of Jerusalem that the Pharisees of Luke's time were opposed as a body to this interpretation? But even if it could be established that the author of Acts was pro-Pharisee, and that Pharisaic opinion largely rejected the covenant interpretation of Pentecost before 70 C.E., would it follow that he would feel constrained to uphold their interpretation of the feast of weeks against an interpretation he may have found in the diaspora? Would those for whom he was writing be the least bit aware of his "changing sides"?

A final objection is that there is no covenant theology in Luke-Acts. To this it must be replied that Luke was able to reproduce covenant traditions in his two-volume work without systematically developing a new covenant theology (Luke 22:20, Acts 3:25). Further, the covenant interpretation of Pentecost could induce Luke to choose the feast for the solemn beginning of the mission of the community, and to employ Sinai imagery in describing the event without at the same time forcing him to adopt a theological theme which he has neither systematically employed nor totally avoided in the rest of his two-volume work.

In brief, the importance of Pentecost among certain Jewish groups, and its natural plausibility for the opening of the mission, probably induced Luke to choose it as the date of the descent of the Spirit upon the apostles.

B. Description of the theophany. Luke describes in some detail what was supposed to have actually happened to the group in the house at the descent of the Spirit.

1. The wind. The first sign of the event that is taking place is the sound of a powerful wind that fills the house where the group is sitting. Luke understandably avoids the word πνεῦμα for wind. But instead of the common ἄνεμος (which occurs eight times in Luke-Acts) he employs πνοή, which appears elsewhere in the New Testament only in Acts 17:25.[64]

[64] Elsewhere in early Christian literature only Pol. 2.1 (in the sense of Ps.

In Greek translations of the Hebrew Scriptures πνοή carries with it the nuance of the creative breath of God.[65] Acts 17:25, διδοὺς πᾶσι ζωὴν καὶ πνοὴν καὶ τὰ πάντα, refers directly to Isa. 42:5: διδοὺς πνοὴν τῷ λαῷ τῷ ἐπ' αὐτῆς (the earth) καὶ πνεῦμα τοῖς πατοῦσιν αὐτήν. This reference from Paul's Areopagus address, generally regarded as a masterpiece of Lukan composition, is probably to be attributed to the author, who has referred elsewhere to this passage in Isaiah.[66] Isa. 42:5 may well have served as the immediate source for Luke's use of πνοή in Acts 2:2. In both passages there is question of God bestowing his πνεῦμα on his people. A distinction due in Isaiah to parallelism suggests a pictorial representation of the activity of the Spirit to Luke.

2. Fire. Acts 1:5 connects the promised coming of the Spirit with the baptism of John, recalling his prediction (Luke 3:16) that the stronger one would accomplish a baptism in wind and fire. Later in the passage, Luke had stressed the visibility of the descent of the Spirit upon Jesus after his baptism (σωματικῷ εἴδει 3:22, to which there is nothing comparable in Mark or Matthew), which is evidently to be linked to the phenomenon described in Acts 2 (ὤφθησαν αὐτοῖς).

The symbolic meaning of fire for Luke is best seen in Luke 12:49:[67] "I have come to cast fire upon the earth, and how I wish that it were already blazing." This is connected to the following passage by an adversative δέ, thus: "I have however a baptism which I must receive, and how I am distressed until it has been completed." In other words, Jesus can send the fire of which he speaks only after his passion and death. The succeeding material speaks of a great division to be

---

150:6); 1 Clem. 21.9 (as God's life-giving spirit; cf. Acts 17:25) and 57.3 (a citation of Prov. 1:23).

[65] It translates *neshamah* fairly consistently (as πνεῦμα translates *ruah*). Various shades of meaning occur: (1) It may indicate the life-giving breath of God: Gen. 2:7; Job 27:3; 32:8; 33:4; Prov. 24:12. (Job 37:10 also indicates the breath of God, but not viewed as life-giving.) (2) It signifies a living creature in Gen. 7:22; 1 Kings 15:29; Ps. 150:6. (3) In Prov. 1:23; 11:13; 20:27, it denotes the intelligence of man. (4) It is used for the life-breath of man: Wis. 2:2; Dan. 5:23; 10:17. (In 2 Macc. 3:31; 7:9, the meaning is similar; the last gasp of a dying man.)

[66] Luke 1:79 and Acts 26:18 reflect Isa. 42:7; Luke 2:31f. recalls Isa. 42:6.

[67] In Acts 2:19 (the Joel citation) fire is one of the signs on earth of the eschatological event. Elsewhere in Luke-Acts it signifies an agent of destruction (Luke 3:9; 9:54; 17:29), or has a nonsymbolic sense (Luke 22:55; Acts 28:5). In Acts 7:30 it designates the burning bush.

effected because of the coming of Jesus. The immediate sequel (Luke 12:54-56) gives an eschatological coloring to the entire passage. Thus the coming of Jesus, and his casting fire upon the earth, will bring about the eschatological judgment among men.

The result of the fire of Acts 2:4 is that each one utters oracles (ἀποφθέγγεσθαι) as the Holy Spirit directs him. The outpouring of the Spirit upon the apostles signifies their prophetic consecration, just as the baptism of Jesus signified prophetic consecration for him.[68] The gift of the Spirit is the fire Jesus came to cast on the earth to effect the eschatological judgment among men through the apostolic preaching.[69]

3. Tongues of fire. The fire that comes upon those in the house appears in the form of tongues (2:3). Then they all begin to speak in different tongues, as the effect of the descent of the Spirit among them. Thus Luke's description of the theophany is in function of the effects that follow.

However, in the light of the connection of the feast of Pentecost with the giving of the law discussed above, it is possible that Luke may have been influenced by imagery used in his time to portray the Sinai event. In *On the Decalogue* 46, Philo's description of the Sinai event has several striking contacts with Luke's description of Pentecost: "A most terrifying voice sounds forth from the midst of the fire pouring down from heaven, the flame being articulated into ordinary speech for the listeners, by which what was being said was made visibly distinct, so that it seems that these things are seen rather than heard." The central thought, the word of God symbolized as fire, is similar to Luke's Pentecost event, and Philo has the same insistence on corporal visibility. It is certainly possible that traditional material similar to that recorded by Philo for Sinai influenced the Lukan presentation of the descent of the Spirit.

[68] I. de la Potterie, "L'onction du Christ," *Nouvelle Revue Théologique* 80 (1958), 225-52.

[69] In the light of the Elijah material in Luke, it is interesting that Sir. 48:1 compares Elijah to fire: Καὶ ἀνέστη Ἠλίας ὡς πῦρ, καὶ ὁ λόγος αὐτοῦ ὡς λαμπὰς ἐκαίετο.

H. Beyer[70] records a later Jewish tradition which represented the voice of God as divided into seventy voices in seventy different languages so that all mankind might hear it. He points out that although this was written down after the Christian period, it could have circulated earlier as a tradition.

Kretschmar[71] traces all of these traditions back to the rabbinic exegesis of Exod. 19, the theophany at Sinai. On the one hand the use of *qol* for thunder (19:16, LXX φωναί), in conjunction with places as Exod. 19:5, Deut. 4:12, led the rabbis to the conclusion that the voice of God was heard at Sinai. When Ps. 29 was employed in commenting the passage, they imagined that the voice of God on Sinai had been split into seven parts. On the other hand, Exod. 20:18 suggested that the people had *seen* God's voice; since fire played such a part in the description of the theophany, Rabbi Akiba declared that the voice of God was visible in flames of fire. While the extant rabbinic passages are later, the tradition itself seems to have been pre-Christian, since it is presupposed by Philo, Acts, and the book of Revelation.

Finally, the image evoked in Acts 2:3 may have an etiological motivation. The imposition of hands is connected in Acts with the bestowal of a ministry (6:6 the seven; 13:3 Paul and Barnabas), and of the Holy Spirit (8:17 Samaria; 9:17 Saul by Ananias; 19:6 disciples of the Baptist by Paul). What would seem more fitting than that the tongues of fire which signified the first bestowal of the Spirit on the disciples to begin the community's ministry should rest upon their heads, a clear image of the imposition of hands?

The description of the theophany in Acts 2:2f. can be sufficiently explained from pertinent imagery with which Luke was probably familiar (some of which he employs elsewhere) without the necessity of postulating an earlier tradition of a "Pentecost event" which he would have used as a source.

C. The effects. The immediate effects of the "baptism in wind and fire" are that all the disciples are filled with the Holy Spirit and begin to speak in different tongues.

---

[70] H. Beyer, *Die Apostelgeschichte*, Das Neue Testament Deutsch 5, 6th ed. (Göttingen: Vandenhoeck & Ruprecht, 1951), 16*f*. See *S-B* 2, 604*f*.

[71] Kretschmar, "Himmelfahrt," 238-43.

1. Filled with the Holy Spirit. The idea of being filled with the Holy Spirit occurs in the New Testament only in Luke-Acts.[72] The influence of the Spirit in the preaching of the apostles is underlined by the insistence in 2:4b that they spoke καθὼς τὸ πνεῦμα ἐδίδου, reminiscent of the Spirit's speaking through the mouth of David in 1:16.

2. Speaking in tongues. A literary repetition (ἐξίσταντο δέ) signals a twofold reaction of the audience to the disciples' speaking in tongues. According to 2:7, Jews from all over the world stand amazed as a group of Galileans speak of the wonderful deeds of God, and each listener understands what is being said in his own language. Sinai traditions may well lie behind this interpretation, which fits in well with the plan of Luke at this point; the voice does not speak to all nations but to Jews who have come up from these nations to the feast at Jerusalem. Universality is foreshadowed; it is not as yet actual.[73]

But quite a different reaction is recorded in 2:12. Observing the behavior of the disciples the listeners exclaim, "They are full of new wine." It is difficult to find a profound theological reason for this interpretation, but there are reasons for believing that it is a perfectly normal reaction of "outsiders" to the phenomenon alluded to by Luke. The same phenomenon occurs at other times after conversions in Acts (10:45f.; 19:6), and is simply described as speaking in tongues (λαλεῖν γλώσσαις). In 1 Cor. 14, Paul seems to take a dim view of the practice of speaking in tongues. Especially significant is his remark: "If the whole church assembles and they all speak in tongues, and ordinary people or unbelievers come in, will they not think you are raving?" (14:23).

What would seem to lie behind the event described in Acts 2 is the religious phenomenon known as glossolalia, which Macgregor[74] defines as "the outpouring of inarticulate sounds under the stress of an overpowering religious emotion, a

---

[72] Luke 1:15 (Baptist), 41 (Elizabeth), 67 (Zechariah); Acts 2:4; 4:8 (Peter); 4:31 (the community); 9:17; 13:9 (Paul). Cf. Luke 1:35 (Mary); 4:1 (Jesus).

[73] According to L. Cerfaux, "Le symbolisme attaché au miracle des langues," *ETL* 13 (1936), 256-59: "Les langues inspirées de la Pentecôte apparaissent comme un signe avant-coureur de la prédication aux Gentils" (257).

[74] Macgregor, *Acts*, 37. Cf. A. Wikenhauser, *Die Apostelgeschichte*, Regensburger NT 5 (Regensburg: Pustet, 1956), 38f.

phenomenon to which there are many parallels in the history of all religious revivals down to our own day." **It is doubtful** that such a thing ever happened in the Jerusalem community; Luke is probably interpolating into the early days of the church an experience common to his own hellenistic milieu.[75]

The twofold interpretation allows Peter to give the true explanation of the event; it is the eschatological outpouring of the Spirit foretold by Joel. Luke has chosen to give a rather favorable interpretation to a rather questionable phenomenon.

D.   The audience. Startled by the unusual commotion, a singular assembly gathers to hear Peter's discourse.

1.   The list of nations. Luke lists the places of origin of those who hear the inspired speaking of the Galilean disciples and who will form the audience for Peter's discourse. The twelve-fold division suggested here will be explained below:

"[1] Parthians and Medes and Elamites, and [2] residents of Mesopotamia, [3] Judea[76] and [4] Cappadocia, [5] Pontus and [6] Asia, [7] Phrygia and Pamphilia, [8] Egypt and [9] the parts of Libya near Cyrene, and [10] visitors from Rome, both

---

[75] Goguel, "Conception," 216-21, argues that two types of religious experience must be distinguished in earliest Christianity. Members of the Jerusalem community remembered the past life of Jesus and looked forward to his future coming. The present was a time of waiting and of living on memories and hopes. For Paul and the hellenistic Christians, however, remembrances—which would be only indirect—of the ministry of Jesus were of lesser importance. They were mainly concerned with the Christ presently reigning in heaven. The latter group would more probably evolve traditions about the pneumatic intervention of Jesus in the community. Cf. Cadbury, "Eschatology," 304.

[76] Textually, ʼΙουδαίαν is secure. It is read in all known Greek mss, and Ropes, *Beginnings* 3, 14, has shown that the few dissenting versions are later attempts to explain the inclusion of "Judea" in the list. Haenchen, *Apostelgeschichte*, 134f., offers several reasons for regarding ʼΙουδαίαν as a later interpolation: (1) It cannot be used in the "counting," since it is joined by τε καί to Cappadocia. Yet codex Bezae reads only καί here; besides, once Haenchen drops Judea, and Cretans and Arabians from the original text, he must count Phrygia and Pamphilia as two groups in order to get twelve—and these are joined by τε καί (except in codex Bezae). (2) No foreign language was spoken there. But Luke takes pains to note that the disciples were Galileans (2:7). He may intend a reference to the special dialect spoken in Galilee at that time (cf. Luke 22:59; explicitly in Matt. 26:73). Or he may intend that one of the languages spoken by the twelve was after all the language of the locality in which the wonder took place. (3) The place is awkward in an astrological list; see n. 83. Haenchen's argument is of course a possible hypothesis. The one presented here attempts to keep the Greek text as it stands.

Jews and proselytes, [11] Cretans and [12] Arabians" [77] (Acts 2:9-11a).

This list is quite similar to one based on astrological geography and found in the writings of Paulus Alexandrinus. The latter wrote in the fourth century c.e., but the list is evidently an archaic one, probably going back to a draft made at the time of the Persian Empire in the fourth century b.c.e.[78] The countries of the world are listed according to the signs of the zodiac as follows, with the equivalent name from Acts in the third column:

Sign	Astrology List	Acts
Ram	Persia	Parthians, Medes, Elamites[79]
Bull	Babylonia	Mesopotamia[80]
Twins	Cappadocia	Cappadocia
Crab	Armenia	Pontus (contiguous region mentioned in Acts 18:2; 1 Pet. 1:1)
Lion	Asia	Asia
Virgin	Hellas, Ionia	Phrygia and Pamphylia[81]
Scales	Libya, Cyrene	Parts of Libya near Cyrene
Scorpion	Italy[82]	Romans
Archer	Cilicia, Crete	Cretans
Ibex	Syria	Judea[83]
Water carrier	Egypt[84]	Egypt
Fish	Red Sea and India	Arabians[85]

[77] For ingenious arguments to explain why the textually secure "Cretans and Arabians" should be regarded as the result of scribal insertion, see H. Conzelmann, *Die Apostelgeschichte,* Handbuch zum Neuen Testament 7 (Tübingen: Mohr, 1963), 26; Goulder, *Type,* 152-58.

[78] Stefan Weinstock, "The Geographical Catalogue in Acts 2:9-11," *The Journal of Roman Studies* 38 (1948), 43-46.

[79] Weinstock, "Catalogue," 44, suggests that a variant form of the list lies behind Dan. 8:20f. in which a ram represents the king of the Medes and the Persians. Luke may have been following another form in which "Parthians" represents an adaptation to a later geographical situation; see J. Brinkman, "The Literary Background of the 'Catalogue of the Nations' (Acts 2:9-11)," *CBQ* 25 (1963), 418-27. The reference to "Medes and Elamites," both mentioned in the Jewish scriptures, may have been added by Luke or his immediate source.

[80] Weinstock, "Catalogue," 44, notes that Babylonia seems to be an earlier term than Mesopotamia.

[81] The double name corresponds to that of the astrology list. The change may well have been made by Luke who understandably avoids mentioning Greece at this juncture, since in Acts "the Greeks" are always set over against "the Jews" (11:20; 14:1; 16:1, 4; 17:4; 18:4; 19:10, 17; 20:21; 21:28). Both Phrygia (16:6; 18:23) and Pamphylia (13:13; 14:24; 15:38; 27:5) figure in the missionary work of Acts.

121

The correspondence is too striking to be accidental. One explanation for the slight divergences may be that Luke knew the list in a slightly different form, perhaps one which he found in some hellenistic Jewish source. Another may be that the names have been chosen in the service of the author's plan for the story of Acts. While the suggestions offered must remain conjectural, it seems quite probable that Luke did make use of a list closely resembling that of Paulus Alexandrinus, a list which seems to have been popular in the early centuries of the Christian era. Luke's purpose in using this list would seem to be to designate the universal nature of the audience at the Pentecost event.[86]

2. Ἰουδαῖοι. Although not read by Sinaiticus, Ἰουδαῖοι is certainly part of the original text of Acts 2:5. In the first place it is favored by the overwhelming textual evidence. More important, Luke does not introduce the Gentiles into the apostolic mission until after Peter's conversion of Cornelius, as was pointed out above. Thus an audience of Jews from all over the world is assembled to witness the descent of the Spirit and to hear Peter's opening address. The narrow bounds of the house in which the disciples were gathered are quickly burst asunder by the power of the Spirit.

E. Resolution of the themes. Luke signaled the consummation of the ἀνάλημψις of Jesus begun in Luke 9:51 by the three-fold ἀνελήμφθη of Acts 1. In Acts 2:1 he opens with the same expression used in Luke 9:51 for the beginning of the ἀνάλημψις: ἐν τῷ συμπληροῦσθαι.[87] The mission of Jesus is over, but a fresh start is heralded in the mission of the apostles.

---

[82] Weinstock "Catalogue," 45, sees this as "definitely a late addition"; "for the Persian Empire (but also for later centuries of Asia Minor) Rome did not exist."

[83] Weinstock suggests that Luke's source was a Jewish writing (46). This may explain why Judea has been substituted for Syria, persecutor of Judea in the second century B.C.E. It is admittedly difficult to explain the place of Judea in the list, but it is probably due to the source and not to Luke himself.

[84] Weinstock notes that Egypt is more correctly in geographical order in the Acts list, and suggests that its place in Paulus' list is due to later astrological speculation which found the sign of the water carrier more suitable to the country of the Nile (45).

[85] Weinstock again suggests that Arabia is the older listing, "and that later it was replaced by the Sea to suit the Pisces [fish] better" (45).

[86] Cf. Sleeper, "Pentecost," 391.

[87] The verb is used only once elsewhere in the New Testament, in Luke 8:23, in the realistic sense of a boat's filling up with water.

The interrelationship of the three themes in now clear: The awaited Spirit comes to enlighten the understanding of the apostles that they may begin the mission given them by the now exalted Jesus.

Conclusion. In Acts 2:1-14a Luke describes the event for which chapter 1 has prepared the reader. It is highly improbable that the account depends on a similar event recounted in early traditions. Individual details, with the exception of the list of nations, probably find their source in the vast fund of information at the author's disposal, and are found elsewhere in his work. The total scene is probably the result of his power to create pictorial representations of key theological themes.[88]

Acts 2:14b-42. The Pentecost Discourse

Analysis of the discourse of Acts 2 has revealed it to be the finest creation of Luke among the early mission discourses in Acts. In its context it interprets and concludes the events of the first two chapters of Acts.

I. *Determination of the sense of the event.* The narration of 2:1-14a is in itself not sufficiently explicit for the development of Acts. Peter's discourse points out the full significance of what has taken place. With the help of the Joel citation, he identifies the prodigy as the eschatological outpouring of the Spirit. The recipients have spoken under the influence of the Spirit, and unusual portents in the heavens and on the earth have accompanied their speaking.

The discourse also connects the phenomenon to Jesus. Before his leave-taking he promised his disciples that they would be baptized in the Holy Spirit (1:5), receiving power to accomplish their mission (1:8). Now Peter explains that Jesus has been raised from the dead by God, of which the apostles are witnesses, and has received the Spirit in such a way that he is able to pour it forth upon his followers (2:33).

II. *Inauguration of the mission.* But Peter does more; he inaugurates the mission of the community. It is not enough to proclaim the vindication and glorification of Jesus. The audience, which has been accused of rejecting this Jesus, realizes that something is to

---

[88] See Ernst Haenchen, "The Book of Acts as Source Material for the History of Early Christianity," *Studies in Luke-Acts,* 258-78.

be done. They question Peter, who replies that they must repent and join the new community assembled in the name of Jesus, and they too will receive the Spirit. The community is no longer a small group of souls huddled together in an upper room; it is a missionary band out to increase its numbers.

III. *Universality of the mission.* No Gentiles are mentioned among the first three thousand converts. But the future universality of the mission is clearly implied.

    A. Universality. In 2:39 there are two indications that the promise extends beyond the audience before Peter:

        1. τοῖς εἰς μακράν. In Isa. 57:19 τοῖς μακράν contrasted with τοῖς ἐγγύς, and Eph. 2:13, 17 explicitly applies this contrast to Jews and Gentiles. That the same contrast is intended here with ὑμῖν . . . καὶ τοῖς τέκνοις ὑμῶν is probable, especially in view of Paul's declaration that he was sent εἰς ἔθνη μακράν (Acts 22:21). To be more specific in Acts 2 was not within Luke's plan.

        2. προσκαλέσηται. In the closing words of Joel 3:5 this verb is in the perfect (προσκέκληται); the future underlines the possibility of salvation for all, because the call of the Lord has not yet been made definitively.

    B. Continuity. But there is no question of neglecting the Jews. Peter's appeal has been made directly to πᾶς οἶκος 'Ισραήλ (2:36) and the Jews are mentioned first as recipients of the promise (2:39).

Conclusion. The Pentecost discourse completes the lines of development of Acts 1–2, and points the way to future evolution:

    A. The opening pericope of Acts describes the definitive conclusion of the earthly mission of Jesus. That the ἀνάλημψις which Jesus began in Luke 9:51 should find its ending only in the second volume is motivated by a desire to link the close of Jesus' mission with the opening of the mission of the apostles in Acts 2.

    B. Continuity between the mission of Jesus and the mission of the community is assured by the leading role of the twelve, a group personally chosen by Jesus and restored after his death by the entire community.

    C. Continuity on a deeper level is assured by the descent of the Holy Spirit on the apostles. The gospel presents Jesus accomplishing his mission filled with the Spirit. Before his leave-taking he promises the disciples that they will be clothed with the power of this same Spirit, a promise fulfilled on the day of Pentecost.

D.   But this continuity entails a discontinuity. In Acts 1 the apostles are evidently not equal to grasping the universal mission that Jesus desires of them. With the coming of the Spirit, however, there is an incipient awareness that the mission is to extend to all those who "call upon the name of the Lord."

Acts 1-2. Thematic in Acts

With the end of Peter's discourse a new section begins, dealing with the life of the primitive community in Jerusalem.[89] Acts 1-2 stands out as a harmonious, self-contained unit. But its influence is constantly observable when, in the remaining chapters of Acts, Luke manipulates his sources in such a way as to depict graphically the gradually expanding apostolic mission according to the plan announced in 1:8.

I.   *Theology of the Spirit.* The Spirit has an essential role in the community in the events of the first two chapters of Acts, a role which is clarified in Peter's Pentecost discourse. In the subsequent speeches there is little mention of the Spirit,[90] and nothing basically is added to what has already been stated [91]—the glorified Jesus has sent the Spirit upon the community to guide and inspire its mission, and all men may receive the Spirit by joining the community in the name of Jesus.

---

[89] Early source criticism detected a change of sources at this point. Dupont, *Sources,* 35-50, discusses the history of this type of criticism since Harnack, judging that it has not attained convincing results. The same break, however, has been claimed by authors following a more nuanced hypothesis than that of two written sources. Thus Lucien Cerfaux, "La première communauté chrétienne à Jérusalem (Actes 2:41-5:42)," *ETL* 16 (1939), 5-31, whom Dupont judges favorably (57-59); and Trocmé, *Le "Livre des Actes,"* 194f. Further literature is given by Trocmé, 194 n. 3, and Dupont, 51-61.

[90] In 5:32 Peter declares that the Spirit aids the apostolic witness to the glorification of Jesus by the Father; in 7:51 Stephen accuses his adversaries of constantly resisting the Spirit; in 11:15 Peter relates to the church in Jerusalem how the Spirit descended upon Cornelius and his companions; in 15:8 Peter reminds the assembly in Jerusalem that God gave the Spirit to the Gentiles as well as to the Jews; and in 20:28 Paul tells the elders of Ephesus that they have been constituted in office by the Spirit.

[91] See Arnold Ehrhardt, "The Construction and Purpose of the Acts of the Apostles," *ST* 12 (1958), 68; reprinted in *The Framework of the NT Stories* (Manchester: University Press, 1964), 89.

The Spirit is however evidently in charge. The Spirit comes upon the community in Jerusalem to strengthen it in persecutions (4:31); inspires Stephen with the courage to face martyrdom (7:55); singles out Barnabas and Saul for their first mission (13:2); inspires the edict of the council at Jerusalem (15:28); directs the second journey of Paul (16:6f.); inspires Paul to start on his way to Jerusalem (19:21); and makes known to him what awaits him there (20:22f.; 21:4, 11).

II. *The Pentecost event.* In crucial moments of the expansion of the apostolic mission, the repetition of the Pentecost event indicates the direction along which the Spirit is guiding the new community:

A. Samaria. Stephen's speech and subsequent martyrdom represent the beginning of the rejection of the community in Jerusalem. Persecuted in the Holy City, many members disperse throughout the towns of Judea and Samaria. The second stage of the mission of Acts 1:8 is about to begin.

It is Philip who brings the word to the Samaritans. He preaches and works signs, healing the sick and driving out demons, and baptizes many in the name of the Lord Jesus. When the apostles in Jerusalem hear of his activity they send Peter and John, who lay their hands on the newly made disciples, bestowing the Spirit upon them. The effects are evidently observable since Simon the magician sees that the Spirit has been given and is impressed enough to want to buy the power of bestowal from Peter. Thus something very similar to the wonderful outpouring of the Spirit on Pentecost has taken place, noted by Luke in his repetition of δώρεα (2:38; 8:20).[92]

This is the first advance of the new community outside of Jerusalem. The apostles there, concerned about the continuity between their work and that of the new missionary, send delegates to investigate. The repetition of the Pentecost event convinces Peter and John that the new work is intended by God.

B. Cornelius. The beginning of the third stage, the mission to the Gentiles, is a good deal more complicated in Acts; Luke knew from his sources, and perhaps at first hand, that great difficulties

---

[92] Elsewhere in Luke-Acts it occurs only in the Cornelius story (Acts 10:45; 11:17) which is considered below.

attended this crucial step in the mission. Peter, protagonist in the incident, is favored with a heavenly vision before he ever meets Cornelius, or even hears of him. The reader is aware that the vision is a legitimatization of the reception of the non-circumcised into the community, but Peter seems not to have grasped its full significance when he leaves for Caesarea. When the sudden descent of the Spirit upon Cornelius and his companions recreates the Pentecost event before his very eyes, however, the apostle understands that these Gentiles are to be received into the community and baptizes them.

The reproduction of the Pentecost event is much more obvious here than in Samaria. If any doubt remains as to its significance it is removed in Peter's explanation of what has happened when he returns to Jerusalem—the Spirit has descended upon these uncircumcised, just as upon the disciples in the beginning (11:15). He quotes the words of Jesus (1:5) referring to the water-baptism of John and the baptism in the Spirit (11:16). Finally he declares that Cornelius and his companions have received the same gift (δώρεα) as the disciples, as a result of their faith in the Lord Jesus Christ (11:17; cf. 10:45).

Since the step taken in the baptism of Cornelius is much more difficult and dramatic than that taken in Samaria there is greater explicitness in the repetition of the Pentecost event; and the agent is Peter, chief of the twelve, which explains the differing role of "those in Jerusalem" in the two incidents. Peter's defense silences the opposition to the admission of Cornelius into the community (11:18). But there is no question as yet of a definite policy of the community with regard to its mission to the Gentiles.

C. The opening of the mission to the Gentiles. Subsequent events draw the new community to a sharp internal crisis. In Antioch, Gentiles are admitted into the community. Barnabas is sent from Jerusalem, and approves the work (11:19-26). Then the Jews of Jerusalem approve Herod's persecution of the new community, and Peter is forced to leave (Acts 12). From Antioch Paul and Barnabas set out on a missionary journey, that eventually sees them turn to the Gentiles. At their return they announce that the door of faith has been opened to the Gentiles.

Meanwhile in Jerusalem the community is plunged into an

127

identity crisis: Shall uncircumcised converts be forced to embrace Judaism by circumcision and the full observance of the law before being admitted into the new community (15:5)? The decisive answer is given by Peter, who refers to the Cornelius episode, when God repeated for the Gentiles the gift of the Spirit he had bestowed upon the Jewish disciples at Pentecost (15:8).

D.   The mission of Paul. After the assembly in Jerusalem Paul undertakes a mission on the mainland of Greece after revisiting Asia Minor. When he returns to Asia Minor an incident occurs at Ephesus which seems to represent approval of his mission. Meeting certain disciples who have received only the baptism of John, he baptizes them and lays his hands upon them. The Spirit descends, producing the same effects as on the day of Pentecost. Underlining the similarity, Luke reports laconically: "The total number of these men was about twelve" (19:7).

Shortly after, the last section of Acts begins (19:21),[93] dealing with Paul's journey to Jerusalem; his trials before the sanhedrin, Herod, and the procurators; and his symbolic death and resurrection in the shipwreck.[94] In the final chapter, this apostle, who has been singled out as the vessel of election to carry the message of Jesus to the Gentiles (Acts 9:15; 13:47; 14:27; 22:21), announces that henceforth the message will be given to the Gentiles, as the Holy Spirit had foretold.

Conclusion. Thus the theology of the Spirit, developed essentially in Peter's Pentecost discourse, dominates the entire book of Acts, and the actual Pentecost event is repeated at each of the key moments in the expansion of the apostolic mission.

Acts 1–2: Theological Prologue

It is evident that Acts 1–2 is a sort of theological prologue, a summary introductory statement by Luke of the theological perspectives which govern the entire work.

I.   The third gospel. Luke has followed a similar procedure in composing the third gospel. At the beginning of the two major sections of the ministry, Luke departs notably from the Markan ordering of

[93] O'Neill, Theology, 62ff., has noted this important division in Acts, similar to the beginning of the ἀνάλημψις of Jesus in Luke 9:51.
[94] Goulder, Type, 36-40.

the material. In 4:16-30, Jesus opens his ministry by preaching to the people of his home town, but is rejected. Yet he goes on his foreordained way (4:30 πορεύεσθαι). In 9:51-56, Jesus is similarly rejected in a Samaritan town; but again he goes on his way (9:56). The final rejection occurs on Calvary. The contacts between the initial and final rejection have been noted above (p. 88, n. 119).[95]

For Luke Jesus is the prophet (and messiah) rejected by the Jews. The theme is stated in his keynote address in Nazareth. Luke 4:16-30 presupposes the incidents that precede it, but it contributes the precise understanding of Jesus as prophet and messiah which explains the unfolding of the subsequent narrative. The theme of rejection is repeated, as the theme in Acts, at the crucial moments of his mission: at the beginning of the ἀνάλημψις, and at the ultimate rejection in Jerusalem.

II. *New theme in Acts.* The theme of the rejection of the bearers of the message of salvation continues in Acts. Stephen, Peter, and Paul are all dramatically rejected, the last named many times, but the message carries on. There is, however, need of new theological perspectives if the reader is to understand the mission of the apostles in Acts. The reason is evident. Especially in the third gospel, the mission of Jesus is to the Jews; yet the church in Luke's time had broken officially with Judaism and consisted largely of Gentiles. How could the apparent hiatus between the two missions be explained to those for whom he was writing? How would it be possible to demonstrate the continuity between the mission of Jesus and the seemingly different mission of the community that claimed to be assembled in and to preach his name?

For Luke, the solution lay in the guidance and prompting of the Holy Spirit whom the glorified Jesus sent upon the disciples. As the mission develops it is the Spirit, on the one hand, who indicates the steps to be taken, and, on the other, the group set up by Jesus, now filled with the same Spirit, who approve them.

III. *Foreshadowing in the first volume.* The universal mission of Acts is not without preparation in the third gospel.[96]

A. Various elements in the opening of the gospel prepare for the

---

[95] The same division is noted by W. C. Robinson, *Weg,* 29.

[96] J. van Goudoever, "The Place of Israel in Luke's Gospel," *NovT* 8 (1966), 111-23.

eventual universal mission which will be instituted by Jesus to be accomplished through his disciples. The Canticle of Simeon (2:30-32) declares that the salvation sent by God in the person of the infant before him is not only for the glory of Israel but as a light for the illumination of the Gentiles. The citation of Isa. 40 placed before the description of John Baptist in the synoptic gospels is lengthened only in Luke to include the verse, "And all flesh will see the salvation of God." The final phrase (τὸ σωτήριον τοῦ θεοῦ) is repeated at the close of Acts when the definitive rejection by the Jews takes place, and the apostolic ministry turns completely to the Gentiles (Acts 28:28).[97] Finally, the immediate cause of the rage of the townspeople against Jesus is his recounting of the examples of Elijah and Elisha, two great prophets who were sent beyond the chosen people to succor Gentiles instead (4:25-27).

B. As noted above (p. 107), only Luke has a sending of seventy disciples, and this (second) sending betrays an awareness of the later missionary endeavors of the community. Assuredly this passage does not explicitly foretell the universality of the mission of the apostles, but when seen in the light of the later developments of Acts it demonstrates that the mission to the Gentiles was according to the principles enunciated by Jesus himself during his lifetime.

Conclusion. Thus the new perspectives delineated in the opening chapters of Luke's second volume have already been prepared by passages in the first.[98]

General Conclusion

As in the third gospel so in Acts, Luke has begun his narrative by a theological prologue which states the basic perspectives from which the book is to be understood, and which then becomes thematic in the succeeding chapters. It is Peter's Pentecost discourse that gives the explicit statement of the theology which lies behind the description of the events narrated in the first two chapters. Thus the discourse of Acts 2 is the Lukan "keynote address," the statement of the theological

[97] Dupont, "Salut," 398-401.
[98] N. Q. King, "The 'Universalism' of the Third Gospel," *Studia Evangelica,* TU 73 (1959), 199-205, refers to a "cryptic" universalism in the third gospel.

position which will explain the subsequent acts of the apostles in the missionary endeavors of the new community that will grow into the Christian church familiar to Luke and his contemporaries.

The Discourse of Acts 3: Sample of Early Preaching to the Jews

Once the author has seen the end in the beginning, by prefacing his work with the theological perspectives attained by reflection on the total process, he is at liberty to present at earlier moments in his narrative theological statements which taken in themselves would be incomplete in relation to his own viewpoint, but which admirably fit the situation into which they are introduced, and taken as a whole reflect the evolution of the thought of the community as it appeared to Luke.

The Discourses of Acts

The discourses of Acts by no means present a homogeneous picture of the Christian community or of its relation to the surrounding world of its time. A rapid survey of the principal speeches will show the genius of Luke who has depicted credibly and consistently the evolution of the self-consciousness of the new community.

1. *Acts 20.* By the time of Paul's farewell address to the elders of the church of Ephesus the community is well enough organized to be referred to as the church of God, whose direction is in the hands of an officially constituted governing class (20:28). The Jews are regarded as enemies of the community (20:19), though Paul foresees other enemies from within who will rise up in the future (20:29).

II. *Acts 17.* After chapter 15 of Acts, Paul occupies the center of the stage with his mission to the Gentiles. Only one long discourse is recorded from this period of activity, but that, delivered in Athens, the cultural center of the hellenistic world, is undoubtedly intended as an ideal statement of the community's beliefs in Greek thought patterns.[99] The basic message presented in earlier

[99] Bertil Gärtner, *The Areopagus Speech and Natural Revelation,* trans. Carolyn Hannay King, Acta Seminarii Neotestamentici Upsaliensis 21 (Lund: Gleerup, 1955), presents a convincing argument to show that the speech is very much in the tradition of Old Testament Jewish tradition. He is further quite convincing when he categorizes the speech as "a specimen of the Disapora preaching which

discourses is there rethought for presentation to the pagans, even to the extent that one of the poets is cited in place of scripture.

III. *Acts 15*. While there is no long discourse in chapter 15, there are two short addresses, one by Peter and one by James, which are of the utmost importance in the development of the book. The purpose of the two speeches is to record the community's solution to the Gentile problem—non-Jews were to be admitted to the community without circumcision and the "burden" of the law. This decision amounts to a first awareness in the self-consciousness of the community of their constituting a body distinct from the Jews (cf. λαός 15:14). It is pronounced by the chief of the twelve and ratified by the head of the Jerusalem community; and it introduces the mission of Paul, which will constitute the second half of Acts.

IV. *Acts 13*. The discourse at Pisidian Antioch is the first speech of Paul in Acts. Significantly it is addressed to the λαός (13:15), as the Jews are then still to be regarded. Paul's discourse marks a critical point in Acts; the Jews in Jerusalem have already rejected the new community in applauding the persecution by Herod (Acts 12). Paul declares that the inhabitants of Jerusalem and their leaders put Jesus to death through their ignorance of the scriptures (13:27), which he insists were read to them every sabbath, and which, it may be inferred, they should have known. This is hardly the ignorance of which Peter speaks in 3:17. At the end of his discourse Paul wants them not to let the message of salvation pass them by, a danger made real by the example of the Jerusalemites before them.

V. *Acts 10–11*. In Peter's speech to Cornelius and his justification of his conduct in Jerusalem, there occurs the first mention of the entrance into the community of non-Jews. This follows the death

---

the Christian Gentile missionaries had taken over from the Jews, and imbued with their own special message" (249). However his attempt to prove the Pauline character of the speech is far less satisfactory. His two basic contentions are: (1) ". . . no item in the discourse clashes with what is otherwise known of Paul's theology" (249); (2) certain details point to early traditions about Paul's actual sojourn in Athens: ". . . namely, the character of the narrative framework, and certain details in the speech, notably its take-off from the altar 'To an unknown God'" (250). The second contention is not substantiated; for a refutation of the first, see Haenchen, *Apostelgeschichte*, 466f.; John T. Townsend, "The Speeches in Acts," *Anglican Theological Review* 42 (1960), 153.

of Stephen, the dispersal of the hellenists, and the mission to the "second-class Jews" of Samaria, and precedes the preaching to the full-fledged pagans in Antioch. There is no question of a policy regarding circumcision, although Cornelius is not circumcised, which fact causes the rumblings heard in Jerusalem against Peter's action (11:3). The community is conscious of constituting a visible social body to which Cornelius is admitted by an external rite (10:47). Moreover, while this body obviously extends beyond Jerusalem (9:31), there is a center of authority in the holy city itself (8:14; 11:1-3, 21). Obviously the way has been opened for the problem which is solved in chapter 15, namely, what exactly is the relation of this new group to Judaism?

VI. *Acts 7.* Stephen's speech takes place in Jerusalem. In the first five chapters of Acts, the favor of the people in general for the new community is frequently mentioned, and even the Sanhedrin has decided to heed the advice of Gamaliel (5:38-40) not to take strong measures against the apostles. But with the incident of Stephen the picture changes. He accuses his Jewish hearers of rejecting Jesus as their fathers had rejected Moses. The action of the Jews in killing Stephen and inaugurating a persecution of the community is tantamount to the second rejection of Moses by the Hebrews described in Stephen's speech. This discourse marks the first crisis in Acts between the Jews (as distinct from their leaders), and the new community;[100] the break in Jerusalem, which becomes definitive in chapter 12, has begun. Stephen's discourse challenges the Jews to take sides, and they reject the message of Jesus.

VII. *Acts 3.* The discourse of Acts 3, then, represents the early preaching of the community to the Jews. It is the sole representative of a kerygma aimed at making the message of Jesus acceptable to the Jews. Peter addresses the λαός (3:12) and indeed all of the λαός (3:11), and offers them the chance to accept the message of Jesus of Nazareth, whom they previously rejected, but through ignorance. There is no community as yet to join; Jesus was sent as servant of God to the chosen people.

The Discourse of Acts 3

The reason for the peculiar non-Lukan, Jewish theological outlook of the discourse of Acts 3 is now explicable.

[100] O'Neill, *Theology,* 72.

I. *Appropriateness of the discourse.* The unusual features of the discourse can be explained by its uniqueness as the only extended, example of the primitive preaching of the new community aimed at making the message of Jesus acceptable to the chosen people as a whole.

   A. Attitude to the Jews and to their leaders. 3:17 is unique in Acts in the excusing of the Jews and their leaders for the rejection of Jesus due to their ignorance. Elsewhere in Luke-Acts the ἄρχοντες play a role hostile to Jesus, and this designation for the enemies of Jesus is peculiar to Luke among the synoptic writers.[101] On three occasions (23:13, 35; 24:20) the ἄρχοντες are said to be responsible for the death of Jesus in Luke, without parallels in Mark and Matthew. Where Mark 10:17 reports that "someone" (εἷς) came to Jesus to ask what he had to do to gain eternal life, Luke 18:18 specifies that he was one of the leaders (τις ἄρχων), and then omits the notation of Mark 10:21, that Jesus looking upon him loved him.

   The same attitude is observable in Acts. The ἄρχοντες gather to persecute Peter and John in 4:5, 8; the community prayer of 4:24-30 cites Ps. 2:1f. to the effect that the ἄρχοντες joined forces against Jesus (4:26); and Paul lays blame for the death of Jesus on the inhabitants of Jerusalem and their ἄρχοντες (13:27).

   Thus, the excusing of the people and their leaders in 3:17 is an extraordinary statement in the totality of Luke-Acts, destined undoubtedly as a *captatio benevolentiae* to win over a Jewish audience.[102]

   B. The distinctive theology. What makes the theology of the discourse distinctive is its Jewishness and the absence of later Christian developments, such as the need for faith in Jesus or the role of the Spirit and the community. But then this is what would be expected in a discourse aimed at a Jewish audience

---

[101] The fourth gospel uses the term in a similar sense in 7:26, 48, but in 3:1 and 12:42 members of this class are said to be favorable to Jesus.

[102] E. J. Epp, "The 'Ignorance Motif' in Acts and Anti-Judaic Tendencies in Codex Bezae," *Harvard Theological Review* 55 (1962), 51-62, has demonstrated an anti-Judaic tendency in codex Bezae, reflected in the change it introduces into this verse. Thus, in place of the B reading οἶδα ὅτι, D reads ἐπιστάμεθα ὅτι ὑμεῖς μέν which sharpens the contrasts between Jews and Christians (you/we) and between the Jews and God (μὲν/δέ, the latter of 3:18). Further, the D-text adds πονερόν after ἐπράξατε, making the action of the Jews a culpable deed (cf. Luke 23:41 where D has πονηρόν for B's ἄτοπον). Cf. Epp, *Tendency*, 42-46.

before the growth of a peculiar self-consciousness on the part of the new community.[103]

II. *Difficulties of the discourse.* Luke has chosen to reproduce traditions which he supposed would characterize the earliest preaching to the Jews in Acts 3; but it is not without a certain amount of difficulty that he has situated the discourse into its present setting.

  A. The link to the miracle. The cure of the lame man which is the immediate occasion for the discourse is done in the name of Jesus. On several occasions the awkwardness of the connecting verse 3:16 has been exposed; moreover, there is no appeal in the discourse to faith in the name of Jesus, which is expected in the light of 2:38 and 4:8-12. What is demanded of the hearers of the discourse is a repentance prompted by distinctively Jewish motives.

  B. The link to the imprisonment. In the two appearances of the apostles before the sanhedrin in Acts 4–5, the chief accusation against them appears to be their teaching in the name of Jesus. Yet the immediate reason for their arrest given in 4:2 is that they are teaching the people the resurrection from the dead in the example of Jesus, which stirs the Sadducean party against them. Understandably, Luke is pursuing a favorite theme, that Christianity is a continuation of what is best in Judaism. Later, in 23:6, Paul is presented as a good Pharisee, suffering at the hands of the Sadducees, who deny the resurrection.

  The transition from the discourse to the arrest and accusation before the sanhedrin is obviously due to the editing of Luke.

Conclusion

It is evident that Luke had an acute awareness of the evolution of the theology of kerygma of the new community. The discourse of Acts 3 represents a first stage in the announcing of the good news, a stage which would later be surpassed, but which already contained certain themes that would be developed later—the messiahship of Jesus and the need for repentance.

[103] Cf. Cerfaux, "Communauté."

Conclusions

The Composition of the Speeches

Investigation has demonstrated that the discourse of Acts 2 is not to be regarded as a sample of early apostolic preaching, but rather as a theological synthesis of Luke, placed at the head of the book of Acts to give the theological perspectives from which the mission of the community is to be understood. On the other hand, there is evidence of primitive material in the discourse of chapter 3, which warrants the conclusion that Luke has reproduced in it traditions which reflect the preaching of the apostles in the period that preceded the beginning of the break with the synagogue.

The divergence in the theological perspectives of the two discourses is significant; but the similarity between them regarding the elements they contain is no less striking. It may be that the one-to-one similarity of the elements is pure coincidence. Yet the care of Luke, which is everywhere observable in his work, and the fact that such a similarity does not exist between any other two discourses of Acts tell against such a possibility.

Since the discourse of chapter 2 is more "Lukan" in vocabulary, style, and thought content than the discourse of chapter 3, and since its structure gives evidence of more polished composition, it seems reasonable to conclude that, having composed a sample of early preaching from primitive traditions, Luke took care in his "keynote address" to up-date the points treated in the discourse of Acts 3 from every point of view.

Thus the conclusion concerning the two discourses: In line with his theological plan for Acts, Luke has composed the discourse of chapter 2 by reworking traditions of the kerygma of the early community, which traditions can be found in more primitive form in the discourse of chapter 3.

The Speech of Acts 3

It by no means follows that the speech of Acts 3 is an actual address delivered by Peter in the early days of the Jerusalem community and simply reproduced by Luke. In the first place, aside from the unusual titles and expressions noted earlier, the vocabulary of the discourse is not notably different from what is generally considered to be that of Luke. Moreover, the connection of the address to the event preceding it (3:16) seems to be the work of Luke. Thus it must be regarded as certain that Luke at least edited whatever materials he received.

Secondly, it cannot be automatically concluded that the traditions which Luke has edited in fashioning this speech stem from the early days of the Jerusalem community. He may, of course, have had access to such traditions; and the Jewish tone of the discourse may indicate a Palestinian (or at least a Syrian) milieu of origin. But to conclude that the material derives from the earliest days of the community would be to go beyond the evidence.

However, if it is decided that the material is *not* in itself primitive, then it must be conceded that Luke intended it to be so. The Jewishness of the speech cannot be doubted, and Luke certainly recognized it as such. That he attributed such a message to Peter in the earliest days of the community is evidence of a far greater grasp of the development of the outlook of the Christian community than that for which he has often been given credit in the past.

The Speech of Acts 2

Similarly it must not be concluded that since Luke created the incident described in Acts 2:1-14a and the subsequent discourse, he necessarily created *ex nihilo* a picture of the community that in no way corresponded to reality. The probability that he made use of early Palestinian traditions in constructing his story of the descent of the Spirit has been presented above. Further, it would seem that the Jerusalem community was already conscious of living in the eschatological times, and that it believed itself to have received the Spirit of God in a special way.

What Luke has done then is to present in pictorial fashion what he believed to be the underlying truth of the beginning of the community. His own conclusion after considering the progress of the Christian community was that its entire development had been providentially directed by God through his Holy Spirit. So that his readers would not lose sight of this reality in reading about the progress of the gospel from Jerusalem to Rome, he so described the beginnings of Christianity that the role of the Spirit would be evident.

The Acts of the Apostles is not a historical account of the foundation and spread of the Christian community. It is an intelligent attempt of a well-informed Christian of the "third generation" to explain how a Palestinian laborer-prophet could reasonably be said to have been the founder of a religious movement that was then making itself felt in the hellenistic world.

Index of Biblical Passages

139

Index of Authors

141

Index of Subjects